About the Author

Reuben Bowd is a Major in the Australian Regular Army and is the son of a career army officer. He was educated at Waverley College and Saint Ignatius College, Riverview in Sydney and is a graduate of both the Australian Defence Force Academy (1998) and the Royal Military College of Australia (Duntroon) (1999). In 2001 he graduated Bachelor of Arts with First Class Honours in History from University College, University of New South Wales at the Australian Defence Force Academy and shared the L.C.F. Turner prize for 'outstanding performance in History'. He has held a variety of positions within the Australian Army and saw service with the Peace Monitoring Group while deployed in Bougainville on Operation *Bel Isi* II and as part of Operation *Anode* in the Solomon Islands.

Major Bowd has published several articles in professional journals and has made contributions in the *Oxford Companion to Australian Military History* (2nd ed.), Oxford University Press, Melbourne, 2008). He is the author of two books: *A Basis For Victory: The Allied Geographical Section, 1942-1946* (Strategic and Defence Studies Centre, The Australian National University, Canberra, 2005); and *Doves Over the Pacific: In Pursuit of Peace and Stability in Bougainville* (Australian Military History Publications, Sydney, 2007).

In mid-2008 Major Bowd completed a Bachelor of Laws (Honours) at the University of New South Wales and is employed as a Construction and Major Projects Lawyer in a major Australian firm (Clayton Utz) whilst undertaking a period of long service leave from the Army.

Disclaimer

This paper represents the author's views alone. It has been drawn entirely from open sources, and has no official status or endorsement.

THE AUSTRALIAN NATIONAL UNIVERSITY

ANU

SDSC

Strategic & Defence Studies Centre

Working Paper No. 414

'Simple Solutions to Complex Matters': Identifying fundamental principles of Alternative Dispute Resolution in the multinational effort to broker a resolution to the Bougainville 'Crisis'

Reuben R.E. Bowd

May 2009

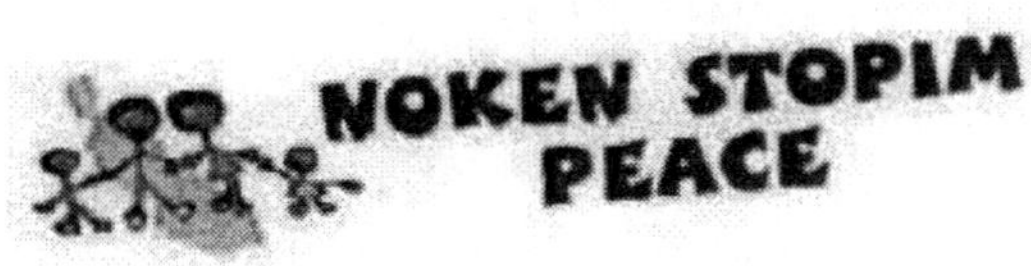

Plate 1
'No-one can Stop Peace'—a sticker produced to advance the Bougainville Peace Process

Published by the Strategic and Defence Studies Centre at The Australian National University, Canberra

National Library of Australia Cataloguing-in-Publication entry

Author: Reuben R.E. Bowd, 1977–

Title: 'Simple Solutions to Complex Matters': Identifying fundamental principles of Alternative Dispute Resolution in the multinational effort to broker a resolution to the Bougainville 'Crisis'

Edition: 1st ed.

ISBN: 9780731554904 (pbk.)

Series: Working Paper (The Australian National University. Strategic and Defence Studies Centre); no. 414

Notes: Bibliography

Subjects: Bougainville Crisis, Papua New Guinea, 1988–.
Dispute resolution (Law)—Papua New Guinea—Bougainville Island.
Bougainville Island (Papua New Guinea)—History.
Bougainville Island (Papua New Guinea)—Politics and government.

Dewey Number: 327.17099592.

Strategic and Defence Studies Centre's Publication Program

Established in 1966, the SDSC is located within the Research School of Pacific and Asian Studies at The Australian National University, Canberra, Australia. It specialises in the study of strategic issues—predominantly in the Asia-Pacific region.

The Canberra Papers on Strategy and Defence series is a collection of monograph publications arising principally from research undertaken at the SDSC. Recent previous Canberra Papers have focused on major aspects of Australian defence policy, disease security in Northeast Asia, ballistic missile defence, cyber-warfare, the complexities of dealing with radical Islam, and aspects of transnational crime.

As at 2006, all papers in the Canberra Papers on Strategy and Defence series are peer reviewed.

In addition, the SDSC also holds a number of 'one-off' publications.

SDSC Working Papers are shorter than Canberra Papers and focus on areas of current research interest to SDSC academic staff or the Centre itself. Topics of previous Working Papers have included Australia's defence policies, Australia's security relationship with Japan, intelligence on Iraq's WMD, Western air power, long-range missiles, instability in the US-ROK alliance, the balance of power in East Asia, New Zealand's defence policies, aspects of future land warfare, and the threat of terrorism on regional development.

Most working papers published between 2003 and 2009 can be downloaded for free from the SDSC publications webpage at <http://rspas.anu.edu.au/sdsc/publications.php>. This page also lists those Centre publications in print that are available for purchase, together with an ordering form.

Publisher

Strategic and Defence Studies Centre
Australian National University
Canberra, ACT 0200, Australia

Tel: +61 2 6125 9921
Fax: +61 2 6125 9926
Email: http://rspas.anu.edu.au/sdsc

Contents

Acronyms and Abbreviations

ADF	Australian Defence Force
ADR	Alternative Dispute Resolution
BAG	Bougainville Autonomous Government
BATNA	Best Alternative to a Negotiated Agreement
BIG	Bougainville Interim Government
BRA	Bougainville Revolutionary Army
BRF	Bougainville Resistance Forces
IOG	International Observer Group
NSP	North Solomons Province (Bougainville)
PMG	Peace Monitoring Group
PNG	Papua New Guinea
PNGDF	Papua New Guinea Defence Force
PPCC	Peace Process Consultative Committee
SPPKF	South Pacific Peacekeeping Force
TMG	Truce Monitoring Group
TPI	Third Party Intermediary
UNOMB	United Nations Observer Mission Bougainville
UNPOB	United Nations Political Office Bougainville

List of Maps, Plates and Tables

Map 1: North Solomons Province of Papua New Guinea (Bougainville)

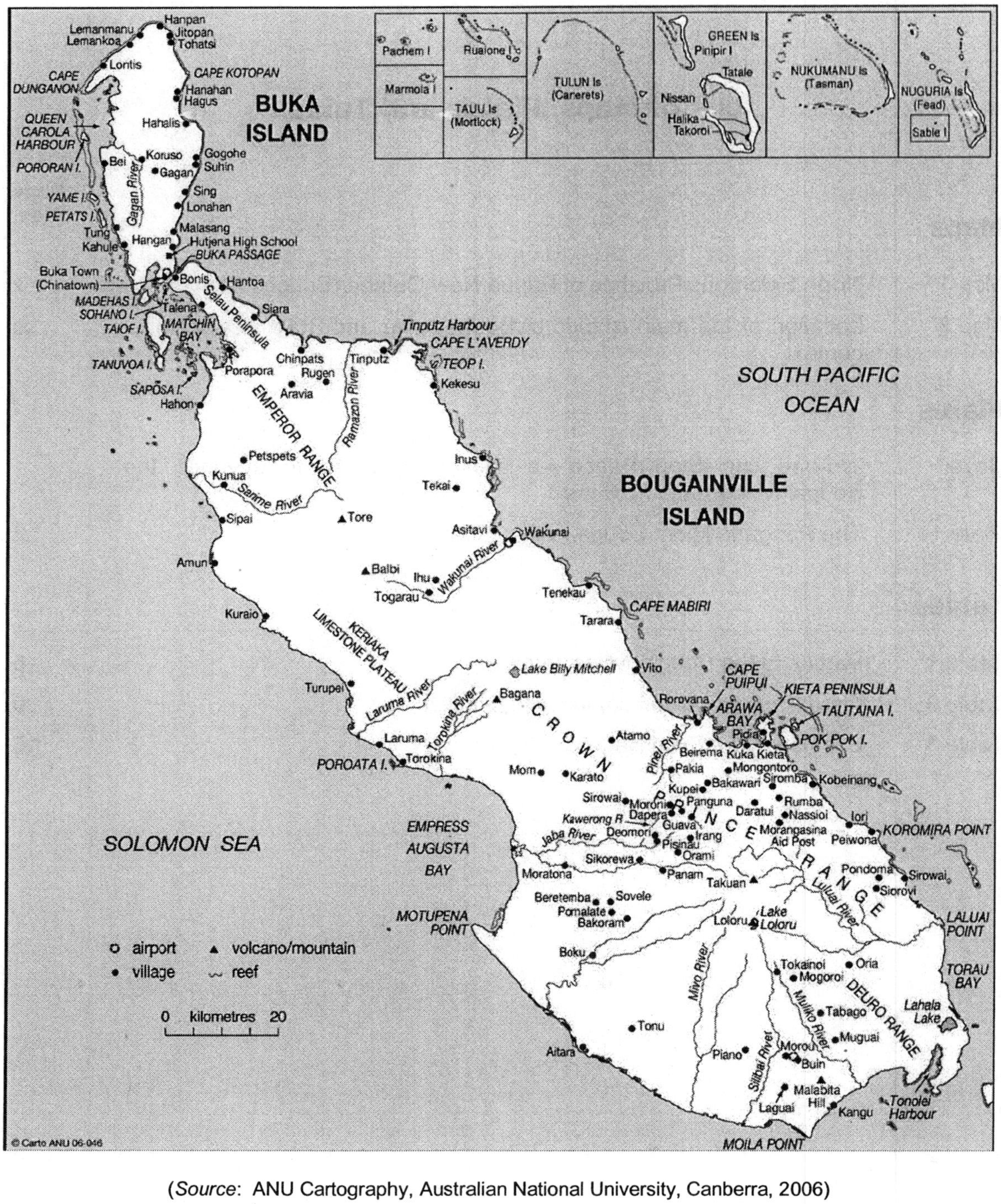

(*Source*: ANU Cartography, Australian National University, Canberra, 2006)

Map 2: Location of the main islands of Bougainville and Buka in a regional context

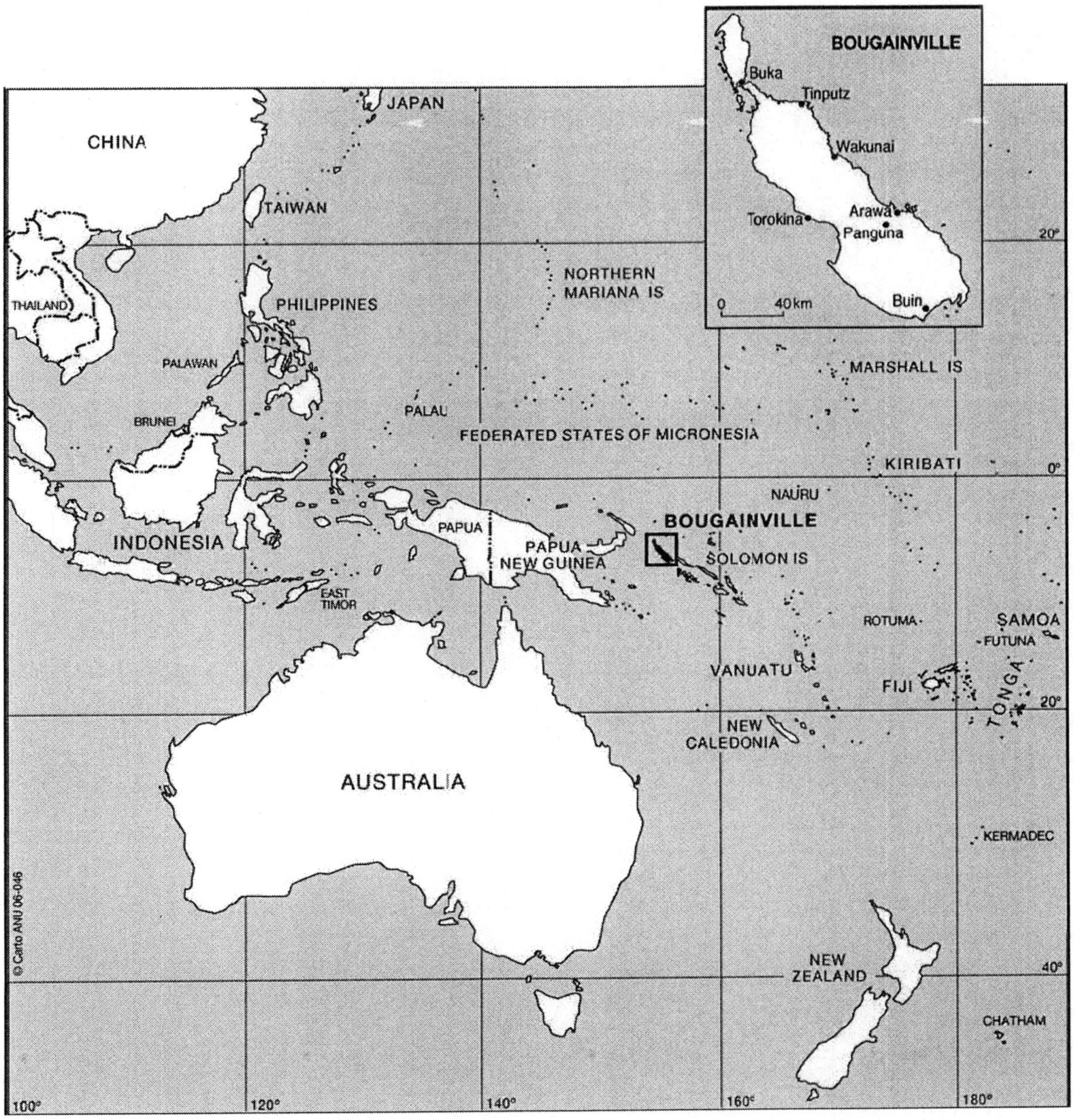

(*Source*: ANU Cartography, Australian National University, Canberra, 2006)

'Simple Solutions to Complex Matters': Identifying fundamental principles of Alternative Dispute Resolution in the multinational effort to broker a resolution to the Bougainville 'Crisis'

Reuben R.E. Bowd

Paddy Palin once said that he was never truly lost. I can only surmise he has never participated in a Peace Awareness Meeting in a remote Bougainville mountain village.

Civilian Peace Monitor at Team Site Wakanai, Central Bougainville, 1999

INTRODUCTION

This paper analyses the multi-national effort to resolve the Bougainville 'Crisis' within an Alternative Dispute Resolution (ADR) framework founded on universal principles applicable to all disputes. Firstly, the dispute will be defined, the parties and their interests identified, and the negotiation process described. The paper will then analyse the two-phase negotiation process that took place in Bougainville by assessing its successes and failures against a variety of factors that are common to all disputes. The problem-solving approach and breakthrough negotiation will be applied to the dispute, and the seven element theory for a successful negotiated agreement (alternatives, interests, options, legitimacy, commitments, communication, and relationship) advanced by the Harvard Negotiation Project will be utilised as a means of evaluating the overall outcome within a conceptual framework. A central theme of this paper is that the universal principles of ADR are just that—they are relevant and transferable to all negotiations, domestic or international.

The Bougainville experience clearly advances ADR as a viable alternative to the employment of combat forces to resolve longstanding international conflicts. In Bougainville, ADR techniques proved to be an unexpectedly powerful primary 'weapon' of conflict resolution that succeeded in the face of conventional military failure. However, the use of ADR on Bougainville was a learned experience accompanied by various challenges that were overcome through gradual refinement and experimentation over a period of almost 20 years.

OVERVIEW: THE BOUGAINVILLE CRISIS[1]

Although geographically and anthropologically part of the Solomon Islands, Bougainville is politically part of Papua New Guinea (PNG). Bougainville and Buka, along with numerous smaller islands and atolls, constitute the North Solomons Province (NSP) of PNG (Bougainville), with a combined land area of about 10 600 square kilometres (roughly one sixth the size of Tasmania).

There are approximately 157 000 people living in the NSP. They are nominally Christian and speak 16 Astronesian and nine Papuan languages that are localised and not commonly understood. Melanesian Pidgin, a product of colonial times, is the primary means of communication.

Plate 1
The Panguna Mine, Bougainville

Until 1989, the NSP exported large quantities of copper, copra, cocoa and timber; an independence movement accompanied by guerrilla fighting has badly affected the economy since then. The catalyst for violence was growing landowner jealousies and dissatisfaction over the environmental impact, compensation and distribution of profits from the colossal Panguna open-cut copper mine and processing facility located high in the mountainous Crown Prince Range of central Bougainville.

The mine's importance to the economy of PNG (during its 17 years of operation) cannot be overstated given that its operations constituted approximately 44 per cent of the nation's exports and generated 17 per cent of the government's internal revenue. Foreign investment also saw Bougainville become one of the wealthiest, best educated and infrastructure developed areas in the South Pacific.

The Bougainville Revolutionary Army (BRA) commenced militant activities in November 1988, targeting local plantations and businesses. The BRA initially stated that its main objective was to obtain increased compensation for landowners who were affected by mining operations. When the Panguna Mine was forced to close in May 1989, the PNG Government declared a State of Emergency and deployed riot police and Papua New Guinea Defence Force (PNGDF) personnel to Bougainville in an ill-disciplined and poorly organised effort to restore order. The BRA subsequently amended its objectives to include secession from PNG. This was entirely unacceptable to the PNG Government: such a precedent could not be allowed in an already fragmented nation.

In March 1990 an *Agreement to end hostilities on Bougainville* was signed between the BRA and the PNGDF that set the conditions for negotiations to commence between the PNG Government and the BRA. It incorporated arrangements for a ceasefire, the withdrawal of PNG Security Forces and the simultaneous disarming of the BRA. This was to be overseen by an International Observer Group (IOG) led by the Commonwealth Secretariat in London. Although both sides initially complied, the BRA reneged on the agreement and took up its surrendered weapons. It also established a political arm, the Bougainville Interim Government (BIG), and proclaimed it to be the legitimate civil authority.

In May 1990 the PNG Government declared 'war' on the BRA and commenced a series of major military operations to recapture BRA/BIG controlled areas. It also imposed a total blockade on government services and supplies to the province. The BRA/BIG responded by issuing a unilateral declaration of independence from PNG on 17 May 1990.

In the total absence of PNG Government authority, the BRA/BIG leadership proved incapable of maintaining law and order and lost control of its factions; these soon became embroiled in local disputes, formed criminal gangs and undertook a campaign of settling age-old scores and the wanton destruction of private and provincial infrastructure. Lawlessness, coupled with hardship caused by the blockade, fostered considerable anti-BRA sentiment and resulted in the formation of the PNG Government-backed Bougainville Resistance Forces (BRF). Some areas of the province, like Buka, even invited a return of the PNGDF. The conflict soon escalated into a protracted civil war with atrocities committed by all parties. An estimated 8000 people (or 5 per cent of the population) would lose their lives in the violence, and the widespread displacement of the civilian population threatened a major humanitarian disaster.

Resolving the 'Crisis' on Bougainville, a trouble-spot on Australia's doorstep, has been at the forefront of Australia's foreign and defence policy since 1988. Furthermore, it constitutes a matter of broader international importance, not least in terms of regional security, but also given the unacceptable cost in human life, and the economic, social and internal security impact on PNG. It was acknowledged quite early that there could be no military solution to the conflict, making a successful negotiated outcome, acceptable to all parties, the only viable option.[2]

PROBLEM-SOLVING AND BREAKTHROUGH NEGOTIATION

The terms 'dispute' and 'conflict' are distinct and distinguishable concepts. A 'dispute' is an argument, debate or quarrel, whereas a 'conflict' involves a struggle or clash over opposing principles that may include resources, ideas, values and inherent human needs.[3] John Burton suggests that although dictionaries may distinguish the two terms, in practice they are incorrectly treated as synonymous in a dispute resolution context. He attributes this to a failure by many to acknowledge 'why and in what respects disputes and conflicts differ in intensity' and he argues that, as a consequence, conventional dispute settlement processes (including adjudication, arbitration, mediation, negotiation and a combination of these) have been inappropriately applied to all situations, whether minor differences (disputes) or major confrontations (conflicts).[4]

To Burton, disputes can be 'settled' by negotiation and compromise, whereas conflicts involve issues that are non-negotiable and cannot accommodate compromise: they must be 'resolved'.[5] Burton objects to the use of conventional methods to 'resolve' conflicts on the basis that they lack the analytical processes necessary to reveal the underlying issues at the source of the conflict. He also believes that 'the treatment of conflicts as though all issues in human relationships are negotiable and subject to compromise, lead to attempts at forced "settlement" within existing institutional and social norms' and therefore temporary solutions.[6]

I am unconvinced by Burton's position on the basis that there exist numerous examples of these so-called 'dispute settlement processes' (like negotiation) being effectively applied to achieve legitimate and lasting outcomes (the conflict on Bougainville is one example). What Burton appears to be advancing is the problem-solving approach to negotiation practised by negotiators like Roger Fisher and William Ury of the Harvard Negotiation Project.

Problem-solving negotiators seek to present disputes as problems that the parties should attempt to resolve to their mutual benefit.[7] Not unlike Burton, 'problem-solving negotiators see compromise as an unattractive solution, not as a goal to be pursued'[8] and warn against overlooking basic human needs (like security) that, if met, can turn an opponent around, or otherwise can block agreement.[9] The objective is to look past personalities[10] and apparently uncompromising and irreconcilable positions (what a party asserts, demands or offers during negotiations) to address underlying *interests* (the needs, desires and fears that drive negotiations).[11] Such action then encourages parties to generate *legitimate options* (solutions) that address all of the *issues* to the mutual satisfaction of the parties—the aim is not to win positions or to gain victories for people.[12] A party should not *commit* to an option unless it is better than their Best *Alternative* to a Negotiated Agreement (BATNA).[13] Effective *communication*, an essential ingredient in all negotiations, is central to the success of the problem-solving approach (a party is more likely to have their *interests* met if these are *communicated* to the other side),[14] which concurrently seeks to enhance the *relationship* between the parties into the future.

To get past 'no' in the most difficult circumstances, negotiators like William Ury employ a five-step strategy (breakthrough negotiation) 'to change the game from face-to-face confrontation to side-by-side problem-solving':

1. *don't react* to an opponent's barriers to cooperation and stay focused on achieving the objective (your *interests*);

2. *disarm your opponent* of their fear, suspicion, defensiveness and hostility so that they listen to you;

3. *change the game* to one whereby *interests*, rather than positions, are being bargained; engage an opponent in problem-solving negotiation and guide them to a mutually satisfactory agreement;

4. *make it easy to say yes* by bridging the gap between their interests and yours; help them save face through *legitimate* options and by making the outcome appear a victory; and

5. *make it difficult to say no* by educating an opponent (perhaps about your BATNA) and make it clear, in a non-threatening manner, what the consequences of a failure to agree will be (third-parties can be effectively employed toward this aim). One should keep in mind the need for an ongoing and constructive relationship by *bringing an opponent to their senses, not to their knees.*[15]

The problem-solving approach, and its subset, 'breakthrough negotiation' are 'all-purpose' strategies that anyone can use with any opponent.[16] They are directly applicable to negotiations conducted to resolve the Bougainville conflict.

BOUGAINVILLE: THE PARTIES AND THEIR INTERESTS

The primary negotiations aimed at resolving the Bougainville 'Crisis' spanned a period of almost 13 years between 1988 and 2001 (negotiations are still ongoing). During that period, some 46 major agreements were negotiated between, and among, the parties (see Appendix). These, along with countless other meetings and exchanges, collectively comprise what I will refer to as the 'Bougainville Peace Process'.

The parties did not remain constant during the Bougainville peace process. As is the nature of protracted conflict, the number of affected or otherwise interested parties increased with time (Table 1 demonstrates this by identifying the various parties involved in negotiations from time to time). However, the parties can be broadly categorised into pro-PNG Government or pro-Rebel political, combatant and other disputants, and interested Third Party Intermediaries (TPIs).

Table 1: Parties to the Bougainville Conflict

Disputants: Political		Disputants: Combatant		Disputants: Other	Third Party Intermediaries (TPI)—Facilitating the Bougainville Peace Process			
Pro-Government	Pro-rebel	Pro-Government	Pro-Rebel		Agreement/Truce/Peace Monitoring and/or Observing	Key Facilitating Nations	International Bodies	NGO
PNG National Government (including the Special State Negotiator) (September 1975–present)	New Panguna Landowners Association (NPLA) (August 1987–November 1988)	Papua New Guinea Defence Force (PNGDF) (1988–2003)	Bougainville Revolutionary Army (BRA) (November 1988–present)	Bougainville Copper Limited (BCL) (April 1972–May 1989) (Note: still a listed Public Company with an interest)	International Observer Group (IOG) (Ghana, Trinidad, Nigeria, Britain, Canada, Sweden and the Netherlands) (12–16 March 1990)	Solomon Islands (1988–present)	Commonwealth Secretariat, London (1990–97)	International Commission of Jurists (1995)
North Solomons Provincial Government (NSPG) (1976–August 1990)	Bougainville Interim Government (BIG) (April 1990–May 1999)	Royal Papua New Guinea Constabulary (RPNGC) (1988–2003)	Me'ekamui Defence Force (MDF) (and BRA 'A' Company) (1997–present)	Local Chiefs and 'Big Men' (1988–present)	Operation BIG TALK and International Observers (New Zealand, Canada and Vanuatu) (27 July–6 August 1990)	New Zealand (1988–present)	United Nations (including UNPOB/UNOMB) (1994–2005)	Moral Rearmament (1995)
Bougainville Provincial Administration in Exile (August 1990–April 1995)		Bougainville Resistance Forces (BRF) (1990–present)		Church Groups (especially the Catholic Church) (1988–present)	Operation LAGOON, South Pacific Peacekeeping Force (SPPKF) Australia, New Zealand, Tonga, Fiji, Vanuatu) (4–20 October 1994)	Australia (1988–present)		Secretary General of Unrepresented Nations Peoples Organization (1995)
Interim Legal Authorities (December 1991–April 1995)				Women's Associations (1988–present)	Truce Monitoring Group (TMG) (Australia, New Zealand, Fiji, Vanuatu) (6 December 1997–30 April 1998)			
Bougainville Transitional Government (BTG) (April 1995–January 1999)					Peace Monitoring Group (PMG) (Australia, New Zealand, Fiji, Vanuatu) (30 April 1998–23 July 2003 (mandate ended 30 June 2003)			
Leitana Council of Elders (1998–present)					Bougainville Transition Team (BTT) (1 July–31 December 2003)			
Peace Process Consultative Committee (PPCC) (October 1998–June 2005)								
Bougainville Constituent Assembly (BCA) (January–May 1999)								
Bougainville Interim Provincial Government (BIPG) (March 2000–June 2005)	Bougainville People's Congress (BPC) (May 1999–June 2005)							
Bougainville Autonomous Government (BAG) (June 2005–present)								

The disputants

For the purposes of this analysis, attention will be focused on the two major disputants in the 'Crisis': the PNG Government, and the BRA/BIG. Anthony Regan reminds us that no party to the Bougainville conflict was 'monolithic'.[17] Instead, complexity is added through the existence of various factions and stakeholders within each camp, possessing vastly different positions (and underlying interests) and perspectives on the major issues. Importantly, the parties commence the negotiation process from fundamentally opposed and seemingly irreconcilable positions. To demonstrate, Sean Dorney (Australian Broadcasting Corporation Correspondent at the Endeavour Peace Talks (August 1990)) observed that the BIG/BRA position

> was more like a demand for surrender ... it obliged PNG to recognise Bougainville's independence, to fund its independent bank, to stock its reserves, and even pay all the future wages of the Republic's public servants. In other words, a nation-sized cargo.[18]

The underlying issues behind each position are discussed later in this paper. However, the BIG/BRA position commences as unconditional secession from PNG and the total withdrawal of PNGDF elements. The PNG Government, on the other hand, regards Bougainville as its sovereign territory; secession is an entirely non-negotiable issue.

Third Party Intermediaries

By 1990, it had become obvious that 'outsiders' could play a vital and constructive role in providing momentum to the peace process and in encouraging the parties to proceed 'in the direction they had already committed themselves to'.[19] Generally, when TPIs are injected into negotiations, the two contending parties will have to give up control over one or both aspects of the negotiation: the *process* (how the negotiation is conducted) and the *outcome* (the result of the negotiation).[20] However, this was not the case in the Bougainville Peace Process—the parties always maintained entire control and ownership of the process and outcome of negotiations. TPIs proved particularly useful on Bougainville: they helped to resolve the dispute by assisting the parties to explore options, helped repair and improve the relationship between the parties and, on occasion, separated the parties to avoid further conflict.[21] However, involving TPIs in the internal affairs of a sovereign nation can be problematic and must be handled as a matter of considerable sensitivity; it was a particularly difficult and embarrassing decision for the PNG Government, which was forced to accept the harsh reality that there was 'no other practical alternative': The PNG Government felt it had lost face by having to involve TPIs in its domestic affairs.[22]

The three best placed TPIs to assist were nation states: the Solomon Islands, Australia and New Zealand. The Solomon Islands played a vital role in facilitating early contact and dialogue between the disputants, although its Government was often criticised by the PNG Government as being overly sympathetic to the Bougainville cause. Because of its historical, political and defence ties to the PNG Government, and the fact that an Australian company owned and operated the Panguna Mine, Australia was at first treated with considerable suspicion by the BIG/BRA. For this reason, Australia's initial involvement in the peace process was low-key, yet instrumental in terms of financial and logistical support. On the other hand, New Zealand was regarded as largely neutral by all of the parties because it was sufficiently detached from the conflict and its origins. New Zealand became a mutually acceptable TPI to all parties and therefore played a critical role as host and facilitator in numerous early interventions.

Other TPIs also played a critical role in the Bougainville Peace Process. The involvement of experts in the field of conflict resolution, negotiation coaches, international observers, peace monitors, and agencies like the United Nations and Commonwealth Secretariat were instrumental in providing legitimacy, security, flexibility and much needed momentum to the negotiations.

THE NEGOTIATION PROCESS

Being an intractable conflict posing a serious threat to international peace and security, the Bougainville 'Crisis' falls at an extreme end of the negotiation spectrum. At first, monadic (one party)[23] attempts were made to resolve or otherwise avoid the conflict. An example was the Bika Report (1988) commissioned by the PNG Government in the hope of appeasing the disputants and thereby avoiding an escalation of the conflict. Additionally, until 1997, both the BRA and PNG Government attempted coercive unilateral resolution through a series of military actions aimed at breaking the stalemate or jockeying to improve their respective bargaining positions, in advance of major negotiations.

However, the Bougainville peace process was overwhelmingly dominated by triadic (involving third parties) attempts at conflict resolution.[24] The process closely resembled *facilitated negotiation*:

> a process in which the parties to a dispute, who have identified the issues to be negotiated, utilise the assistance of a neutral third party (the facilitator), to negotiate the outcome. The facilitator has no advisory or determinative role on the content of the matters discussed or the outcome of the process, but may advise on or determine the process of facilitation.[25]

Facilitation is therefore a process that 'requires the presence of a third party whose role it is to inject some degree of lateral thinking into multi-party disputes. This has the purpose of helping the parties to agree on a common course of action to resolve the problem'.[26] Third party involvement can be minimal (limited to the provision of logistical support to the process) or extensive (offering advice to the parties).[27] The Bougainville Peace Process is useful because it demonstrates both extremes of the facilitated negotiation spectrum. It also provides examples of the variety of roles that third parties can play in a dispute resolution process. Three (of many supporting) examples are offered in table 2 on page 9:

Table 2: Third Party Roles for Coping with Conflict

Range of Third Party Roles	Example	Who Played the Third Party Role?
Primarily process orientated roles (such as hosting a diplomatic conference)	The Endeavour Peace Talks hosted by the Royal New Zealand Navy aboard military vessels (1990) with civilian International Observers—New Zealand support was limited to hosting the peace talks.	New Zealand Government International Observers: Canada, New Zealand and Vanuatu
Mixed process and substantive roles	The SPPKF deployed following the Honiara *Ceasefire Agreement*. The SPPKF facilitated logistic support and security to enable the conduct of the Arawa Peace Conference (1994).	Governments of Australia, Vanuatu, Fiji and Tonga (Note: the Solomon Islands Government facilitated and chaired the talks that resulted in the Ceasefire Agreement and Chaired the Arawa Peace Conference).
Primarily substance orientated roles (monitoring compliance after agreement)	Compliance with the *Burnham Truce* (1997) was monitored by a regional Truce Monitoring Group (TMG). Monitoring compliance with the *Lincoln Agreement* (1998) was the responsibility of a PMG and the United Nations through its Political Office/Observer Mission on Bougainville.	Governments of Australia, New Zealand, Vanuatu and Fiji. United Nations

(Source: R. Fisher, *Beyond Machiavelli: Tools for Coping with Conflict*, Penguin Books, New York, 1996, p. 124)

Neutrality and conflict resolution

Conflict resolvers have traditionally placed considerable importance on the 'neutrality' and 'impartiality' of TPIs. To Bernard Mayer, this emphasis is misplaced because it denies the fact that 'the commitment of third parties is to help people work through a conflict in a wise way and in keeping with a certain set of values or standards, but not necessarily without taking sides or having one's interests at stake as well'.[28] I also disagree with the definition of the National Alternative Dispute Resolution Advisory Council that emphasises the requirement for facilitator *neutrality*—to me, third party neutrality is not essential; it is a myth.[29] Likewise, Laurie Nathan suggests that, in international mediation, an emphasis on third-party impartiality reflects 'an ideal that is not fully attainable'.[30] Although mediators must be non-partisan and treat all sides fairly, William Smith[31] argues that third party interventions in international disputes differ from their domestic counterparts, because,

> whereas the impartiality of mediators in domestic settings stems from the fact that they have no extended relationship with the parties and no interest in the dispute beyond its peaceful resolution, states have little motivation to mediate in international conflicts other than because they have a relationship with the adversaries and an interest in the details of a settlement. International mediators are thus probably always biased to some degree.[32]

Not unlike conventional dispute resolution, the issue of third party neutrality becomes less important in situations where neither party raises an objection to the intervention and therefore willingly enters into the process.[33] The Challenges Project identified that gaining the consent of the parties to a conflict was 'the ultimate factor in determining the success of a peace operation' (a third party intervention).[34]

In Bougainville, the issue of third party neutrality was particularly important to both parties in the early stages. However, neutrality was viewed in the sense that an acceptable third party was 'omnipartial' (on both peoples side at the same time).[35] As the parties developed trust and confidence in the process, the issue became less prevalent; thereby allowing states like Australia, that were previously viewed with considerable suspicion by the Bougainville side, to take an increasingly active role in facilitating a resolution to the conflict.

Phases in the Bougainville Peace Process

A detailed analysis of the Appendix reveals the existence of two distinct phases in the Bougainville negotiation process: (1) preliminary efforts to reach a negotiated settlement (1988–June 1997); and, (2) the development of a comprehensive negotiation process, reconciling issues and generating a 'yesable' proposal that is sufficient, realistic and operational (July 1997–2001).[36]

Phase 1: Preliminary

This phase is often unfairly judged a failure because it was characterised by successive unsuccessful attempts at resolution over a nine-year period. In most conflicts, some form of resolution is required before there can be effective negotiation—'participants who are in conflict, who oppose and distrust each other, do not have a good basis for negotiation. Until there is at least a minimum level of resolution of the relationship between them, negotiating may be frustrating and ineffectual.'[37] For this reason, phase 1 was anything but a failure. It 'built vital experience, contributing to relationships between key actors on all sides' and developed much needed confidence in the negotiation process.[38]

The following observations assist in explaining why a resolution to the conflict proved unattainable during phase 1; it should be noted that most, if not all, of these reasons regularly affect the outcome of conventional negotiations:

- ***No 'ripe' moment:*** The predominant explanation for a failure to achieve an early resolution was the non-existence of an optimal (or 'ripe') moment for negotiations to take place—in serious conflicts, negotiation will only succeed if it can capture a particular moment 'when the adversaries, for a variety of reasons, appear most amenable to change'.[39] A 'ripe' moment typically presents at a point when the parties reach a 'mutually hurting stalemate' which brings them together in the hope of achieving a lasting settlement.[40] Before 1997, such a 'ripe' moment had not yet materialised. The parties had not exhausted the hope of resolving the conflict through force of arms.

- ***Perception gap:*** A dangerous perception gap existed between the parties whereby each believed they had 'won' violent exchanges outside of the negotiation process, without acknowledging that the other side held the same perception.[41] Therefore, there was an unwillingness to negotiate on the main issues, including the future political status of Bougainville, because both sides perceived that they held the strategic high ground whereby they could 'take all' without negotiation. This gap was eventually bridged with the passage of time.

- ***Failure to involve all parties:*** Before 1997 not all interested groups and major stakeholders were recognised or represented as equal partners in the peace process.[42] With the passage of time, new parties like the BRF emerged but were incorporated into negotiations relatively late in the process.[43] Hence, not all of the parties were signatories to the early agreements, and were therefore not bound to their commitments.

- ***Lack of authority to settle:*** The parties to agreements often lacked any authority to settle. For example, BIG/BRA leader Francis Ona refused to personally participate in any negotiations or genuinely delegate authority to his representatives who did participate.[44] Likewise, the PNG Government delegations could not settle without the approval of parliament. This situation did not improve until 1997, when BIG/BRA 'moderates' moved to disassociate themselves from 'hardliners' like Francis Ona. Likewise, the National Government adopted a bi-partisan approach (that incorporated the creation of a Special State Negotiator) toward the negotiation process. This approach provided greater certainty to commitments. The importance of 'moderate' leadership cannot be overstated: 'peaceful outcomes are more likely when the leaders of the parties to the dispute are moderate in their words, actions, and policies, make conciliatory gestures, and seek bilateral or multilateral negotiations and bargaining to resolve their issues of dispute.'[45]

- ***Spoilers:*** Resolution is more likely to be effective if no factions (within each community) remain committed to the continuation of violence.[46] This was not the case in the early years of the Bougainville conflict. Genuine and honest efforts by the PNG Government to resolve the conflict were often undermined by its own agencies—particularly the security forces that feared losing face if others succeeded where the military could not. Sometimes these agencies deliberately violated agreements through unilateral and unauthorised activities aimed at ensuring agreements did not succeed. Likewise, the BIG/BRA refused to participate in significant peace efforts such as the Arawa Peace Conference (1994), and therefore undermined the process.

- ***Motivation not to negotiate:*** In the early years of the dispute there were hidden agendas and undisclosed motivations on all sides that worked against achieving a lasting agreement. On the PNG Government side, there was strong opposition to negotiations and a military solution to the 'Crisis' was preferred. Furthermore, some of the negotiations may be criticised as mere grandstanding. For example, the *Endeavour Accord* (1990) came at a particularly important time for the PNG Government because the leader of its delegation, Sir Michael Somare, was a candidate for President of the UN General Assembly. It was hoped that securing a negotiated settlement on Bougainville would advance his election to that post. When it became apparent that Somare would not be elected, key PNG Government figures lost enthusiasm for the agreement and those in favour of a military solution regained ascendancy.

- ***Misuse of process:***[47] The negotiation process was initially misused by both parties. It was inappropriately utilised as an opportunity to test resolve and as a 'fishing expedition' to gain information that might strengthen respective positions. Furthermore, a detailed analysis of the early negotiations on Bougainville demonstrates that BRA/BIG and PNG hardliners did not approach the process with a spirit of goodwill and often had little, if any, intention of implementing agreed outcomes or commitments. This further fuelled distrust between the parties and proved an obstacle to future negotiations.

  The Challenges Project identifies misuse of process as a major reason for failed attempts at achieving the peaceful political settlement of disputes. For success to be achieved the parties must genuinely want to resolve their differences peacefully. However, Dennis Jett observes that:

  > Many parties in civil wars sign peace agreements for tactical reasons without intending to live up to their obligations. Movements and leaders may define the stakes in all or nothing terms.

> They may be willing to sign and implement an agreement if it suits their immediate interests, but will defect if the agreement will not bring them complete power.[48]

This observation certainly holds true for the early experiences of negotiations conducted between disputants in the Bougainville conflict.

- ***Focusing on positions rather than interests:*** Roger Fisher remarks that 'in a conflict situation, particularly if it has involved violence, feelings are likely to be more important than thoughts. Participants ... are more apt to be ready for battle than for cooperatively working together on a common problem.'[49] This was the case on Bougainville where the parties proved incapable of reaching an early resolution because they were focused on entrenched positions rather than underlying, and often reconcilable, interests. Furthermore, for negotiations to succeed parties must genuinely be 'willing to communicate' and there must be at least some matters that are negotiable.[50] The presence of non-negotiable issues (such as secession) further entrenched the parties in their respective positions.

- ***Inappropriate reliance on both 'sticks and carrots':*** 'Sticks' are used to 'make the present course more unpleasant' while 'carrots' are designed to make a 'future alternative more attractive'.[51] The PNG Government used a 'stick' (the Bougainville blockade) at a time when 'engaging in dialogue' could arguably have been more productive. Likewise, 'carrots' aimed at avoiding the conflict (like the Bika Report that promised economic incentives to the rebels) proved ineffective because they did not address the root causes of the conflict.

- ***Inadequate documented outcomes:*** Agreements need to be adequately documented.[52] The early agreements reached between the parties were open-ended and not comprehensive, clear, well planned or durable.[53] This made them difficult to enforce, and ambiguous when it came to confirming commitments made by each party. For example, the BRA/BIG and the PNG Government both insisted that the first ceasefire agreement (1990) was to be produced as a one-page document. Later in the Bougainville Peace Process this ceased to be a problem. For example, the *Bougainville Peace Agreement* was a 75-page document that was comprehensive and enforceable.

- ***Well poisoning:***[54] To add pressure to the negotiating environment, both the PNG Government and the BRA/BIG regularly used the media quite ruthlessly to accuse each side of atrocities or insincerity, in the hope of enhancing their respective positions. The parties eventually developed a level of trust, confidentiality and negotiating maturity that saw the media excluded from sensitive talks. Later in the process, the parties enhanced their relationship by issuing Joint Press Statements following negotiations.

The first phase of the negotiating process (1988–97) effectively satisfied the first two challenges of Breakthrough Negotiation: (1) both sides learned to overcome barriers to cooperation, and to control their *reaction*s in the face of adversity, and (2) a favourable negotiating climate had slowly emerged whereby both parties were sufficiently *disarmed* of their initial fear, suspicion, defensiveness and hostility to effectively participate in problem-solving negotiations.

Phase 2: Developing a viable process, reconciling issues and generating a 'yesable' proposition

Phase 2 of the Bougainville peace process (1997–2001) is characterised by a number of significant breakthroughs that culminated in a binding agreement between the parties. The negotiations demonstrate the flexibility of ADR processes and their universal application to all manner of disputes. The successes achieved can be attributed to the following:

- ***An initial focus on establishing a process rather than on outcomes:*** Between July 1997 and April 1998 the focus of negotiations was on the establishment of a robust negotiation process that would serve the parties into the future. The critical issues, including the political future of Bougainville, were set aside and it was mutually agreed that they would be addressed once the process was securely established.[55] A truce and ceasefire were negotiated (to be supervised by third-party monitors) that created a secure environment conducive to problem-based negotiation.

- ***Joint Negotiating Position:*** In December 1999, the Bougainville Delegation presented a Joint Negotiating Position to the PNG Government reflecting the common view of all interested parties on the Bougainville side. This clarified for the PNG Government what the Delegation hoped to accomplish, and for what purpose.[56]

- ***Importance of neutral venues:*** The availability of neutral venues, where negotiations could be conducted in a secure environment, was enormously important. For example, in 1997 the New Zealand Government offered the parties Burnham Military Camp, near Christchurch, as a venue. To the Bougainvilleans tight security and the military atmosphere of the camp helped to reduce fear and mistrust that had haunted them over decades. This enabled the parties to speak freely about the pain and frustration of the war. In Bougainville in 1997 this type of session would have led to more violence, but in Burnham Bougainvilleans could take advantage of neutral ground.[57] By April 1999 the relationship between the parties had developed to a point where a neutral venue was no longer an important issue. All parties felt secure enough to agree that future negotiations should take place in Bougainville or PNG.

- ***Reconciliation:***[58] The Bougainville side conducted a series of group negotiations aimed at reconciling its own factions and internal divisions. This was critical because it was essential that all Bougainvilleans acknowledge that 'the war had divided them, and without a commitment to each other and the entering into a process of reconciliation and unity at all levels of the community; there could be no possible hope of ever achieving peace with Papua New Guinea'.[59] As a significant symbolic step toward reconciliation, two prominent Bougainville leaders co-chaired the July 1997 all-Bougainville talks.

- ***Development of trust:*** Trust and understanding gradually fostered between the belligerents and materialised in actions that included apologies and unconditionally constructive acts of good faith.[60] For example, following the all-Bougainvillean talks at Burnham in July 1997, the BRA agreed to release five PNGDF soldiers who had been captured in September 1996. This was a gesture of gratitude to the PNG Government for agreeing to allow the parties to meet in New Zealand. In response, the PNGDF guaranteed safe passage for Bougainville leaders returning after the talks.

- ***Venting:*** Alan Limbury advances two essential phases to a successful negotiated settlement: the 'who did what to whom' (venting) phase; and the 'what's it going to take to fix it?' (solution) phase.[61] He suggests that the chances of reaching a successful settlement are compromised when the first phase is rushed, or otherwise ignored. This is because 'people are frequently unable to focus on possible solutions until they have finished telling the story of how they got to where they are now'.[62] Early attempts at resolving the Bougainville Crisis suffered as a result of neglecting Limbury's first phase. Sufficient emphasis was not placed on allowing the parties to tell their story, thereby preventing effective communication and the exploration of viable solutions. The Bougainville Delegation, in particular, required an opportunity to be heard, and to vent their anger, before they could proceed to explore possible solutions that would meet the interests of all parties. The different factions needed to be assured that the PNG Government, and their own side, understood their concerns and the difficulties they had faced.[63] Taking into account cultural considerations, the talks conducted at Burnham in July and October 1997 incorporated a two-day open session known as a 'Taraoting' (literally translated as 'vomiting session') wherein all representatives freely expressed their views and concerns and had a genuine opportunity to tell their story before proceeding to negotiate.[64]

- ***Dispute resolution training:*** Significant progress can be attributed to 'capacity-building' individuals who assisted the peace process by training the parties to more effectively participate as negotiators.[65] For example, in June and July 1997, two Australian lawyers ran a negotiating skills workshop for the BIG/BRA in Honiara and for the Bougainville Transitional Government in Buka to enhance their participation and communication skills in preparation for the Burnham talks.

- ***Timely intervention of TPIs:*** Consultation at some meetings was only achieved through third-party facilitation. For example, at times 'shuttle-diplomacy' was required by Australian and New Zealand diplomats in order to bring the parties together. On some occasions (like the Lincoln talks of January 1988) participants refused to talk and it took the intervention of trusted TPIs (including individuals like the former New Zealand High Commissioner to PNG, John Hayes) to get the parties talking.[66]

- ***Creation of a Dispute Resolution Procedure:*** William Ury states that 'guarantees offer you a *final* resort if your opponent breaks the agreement—but they don't give you a *first* resort. For that you need to establish in advance a dispute resolution procedure.'[67] The establishment of a Peace Process Consultative Committee (PPCC), comprising representatives of all affected parties and chaired by the United Nations, was such a procedure that all parties agreed would be a *first resort* to resolve issues concerning compliance with the various peace agreements.

- ***Presence of non-warring parties (civil society):*** The increased presence of affected non-warring parties, including church and women's organisations was critical to the negotiation process. In particular, women 'mediated between all sides of the conflict and contributed to bringing the parties together'.[68] The voice of Bougainville's women was incredibly influential (Bougainville is a largely matriarchal society). The presence of women's groups at critical negotiation sessions brought home the full impact of the conflict and its cost to civil society. It became increasingly difficult to justify continued violence and failed negotiations when mothers, sisters, daughters and wives of combatants, who had experienced considerable hardship throughout the conflict, actively petitioned their men for peace.[69]

Phase 2 of the Bougainville peace process, that ended with the *Bougainville Peace Agreement*, met the final three challenges facing breakthrough negotiators: (3) The *game had been changed* to be conducive to problem-solving (focusing on *interests*, rather than positions) and a mutually satisfactory agreement was achieved; (4) The interests of the parties were bridged by legitimate options that made it *easy for both parties to say yes* (win/win) and to save face with their respective constituencies; and, (5) It became *difficult to say no* because of the unfavourable BATNA of both parties, the expectations and encouragement of third-parties and the involvement of affected non-warring elements of civil society that were weary of the conflict and desired peace.[70]

THE FINAL ANALYSIS: APPLYING THE HARVARD SEVEN ELEMENTS

In October 1997, the *Burnham Truce* was signed by the parties to declare an end to hostilities, a commitment to establishing a clear negotiation process to determine Bougainville's political future, and a ceasefire to be supervised by a neutral TMG. By January 1998, the TMG had been deployed and the parties reached another significant milestone, the *Lincoln Agreement* that was subsequently implemented through the *Arawa Agreement* (April 1998). The *Arawa Agreement* provided for a permanent and irrevocable ceasefire and for a transition of the TMG into a PMG. It also established the PPCC, with a sub-committee on weapons disposal, to resolve disputes concerning compliance with the agreement. The PPCC comprised representatives of all parties, and was chaired by the Director of the United Nations Political Office Bougainville (later the United Nations Observer Mission Bougainville or UNOMB). Most importantly, the *Arawa Agreement* triggered the commencement of the negotiation process on the central issue in dispute—the future political status of Bougainville—an issue that was finally resolved through a comprehensive *Bougainville Peace Agreement* in August 2001. Table 3 demonstrates the final negotiated outcome agreed upon as a settlement to the Bougainville 'Crisis' by showing the mutually acceptable options adopted as legitimate solutions to the underlying issues behind each parties' position.

Table 3: Evaluating the Final Negotiated Outcome

Issue	Party	Starting Position (1988)	Agreement reached to settle the dispute: *Bougainville Peace Agreement* (30 August 2001)
Issue 1 (Bougainville's secession/greater autonomy)	Bougainville	Immediate Secession from PNG	• Bougainville will be granted a high level of autonomy within PNG via amendments to the PNG Constitution to establish a Bougainville Autonomous Government (BAG). • Bougainville will establish its own Constitution, courts, police and public service. The PNG Government will remain responsible for taxation and the provision of essential services (ie telecommunications, defence, post, foreign affairs and taxation until self-dependence is achieved).
	PNG Government	Secession is not, and never will be, negotiable	• The BAG will be elected and established once the UNOMB confirms that the security situation on Bougainville is stable enough for the conduct of elections. • The people of Bougainville will freely decide the matter of secession from PNG via a referendum on independence to be held within 15 years (and not less than 10 years) of the election of a BAG (unless the BAG decides not to conduct such a referendum). • Amnesty and pardon for those involved in the conflict. • Until the BAG is established, the parties will consult to resolve any disputes that may arise and agree to engage a mutually acceptable third-part if required.
Issue 2 (Security situation on Bougainville)	PNG Government	Bougainville is PNG sovereign territory and the Security Forces must remain. The BRA must disarm.	• Phased withdrawal of PNG Security Forces to coincide with an improving security environment on Bougainville (under the supervision of the UNOMB and the PMG). • PNG Government to establish a Bougainville-specific Police Force to maintain law and order.
	Bougainville	Total withdrawal of PNGDF and Security Forces from Bougainville and a right to bear arms	• The BRA and other factions will disarm in accordance with a three phase Weapons Disposal Plan formulated by the PPCC (surrender of arms, containment of weapons and verification by the UNOMB). The final phase will be a decision on the final fate of the weapons by the PPCC following UNOMB verification. • Until the BAG is established, the parties will consult to resolve any disputes that may arise and agree to engage a mutually acceptable third-part if required. • The PPCC reaffirms commitment to the permanent and irrevocable ceasefire.

(*Source*: Reuben R.E. Bowd)

The Harvard Negotiation Project's seven-element diagnostic checklist can be used to evaluate the effectiveness of the final negotiated outcome of the Bougainville Peace Process:

- ***Interests:*** A negotiated outcome should satisfy the interests of both parties, at least better than if there were no agreement.[71] The underlying interests behind the respective positions of the disputants in the Bougainville 'Crisis', although initially opposed, did not prove irreconcilable. To the Bougainville side, it was important that the issue of secession be addressed, and that concessions be gained toward the achievement of greater autonomy for the NSP. It was also in its interest to remove PNG Security Forces from the province. For the PNG Government, the fundamental issue was ensuring that Bougainville did not achieve independence by force of arms. To allow such a precedent to occur would serve as an incentive to various secessionist movements in other parts of PNG and would undermine the authority of the National Government. It was also critical to the Government's security interest that the militants be disbanded and disarmed and to strike a compromise that would allow all sides to part with dignity, and their interests sufficiently satisfied. The shared interest of both parties was the achievement of a lasting peace which was being demanded by their war-weary constituent base upon whom all of the leaders themselves relied to maintain power.

- ***Options:*** The best negotiations are those in which a number of possible options (solutions to issues being negotiated) have been explored.[72] Over the course of the peace process, numerous options were explored to resolve the issue of secession and the security situation in Bougainville. The option adopted constitutes a 'yesable proposition' that is realistically achievable, sufficiently meets the interests of all parties and has an operational effect in that it tells the parties who will do what and when.[73]

- ***Alternatives:*** Alternatives are other ways of accomplishing interests. Interests can be satisfied through either a negotiated agreement (adopting an option as a solution to interests) or through a BATNA that is independent of the negotiation process. Parties should walk away if they cannot adopt an option that is better than their BATNA.[74] The PNG Government and the Bougainville leaders had no viable BATNA available as an alternative to a negotiated outcome. Even the option of returning to military action was no longer viable to either side. Both sides acknowledged that they were unilaterally incapable of breaking the stalemate through force of arms, and that their constituent base longed for peace.

- ***Legitimacy:*** Negotiations invariably involve reconciling competing interests. Legitimacy involves criteria of fairness measured by some external objective principle or standard. These principles and standards assist the parties to choose between their options. They also assist both parties to justify to their constituents why they accepted a negotiated agreement.[75] The agreement negotiated invariably meets several objective criteria for legitimacy. The PNG Government departed the process satisfied that its withdrawal of forces, and the granting of increased autonomy, was not an unreciprocated concession but was directly linked to the compliance and disarmament of the Bougainville militants and to achieving a state of security determined by the UNOMB—an independent third party.[76] The use of the PPCC (which comprised representatives of all disputants and was chaired by the UNOMB) and the PMG to oversee compliance with the peace agreements also gave the process legitimacy. Providing the PNG Government a minimum of 10 years 'breathing space' prior to a Bougainville referendum on independence was also justified to the Bougainville side using legitimate external criteria. This element of the agreement guaranteed the Bougainville people a future opportunity to exercise their collective rights within a lawful and democratic framework, whilst also providing time for the NSP to gain a sufficient level of reconciliation, political and financial self-reliance to legitimise its claim to independence.

- ***Communication:*** With good communication, negotiation makes it easier for parties to deal with each other in the future.[77] During over a decade of conflict, and numerous negotiations, the parties had clearly articulated their perceptions and interests to the opposite side. They also developed sufficient confidence to communicate directly with each other. The PPCC, TMG and UNOMB were all mechanisms through which the parties could check whether what was understood to have been agreed is in fact what eventually happened.

- ***Relationship:*** A successful negotiated agreement will improve the relationship that exists between the parties. 'Unconditionally constructive' steps should be taken to improve the relationship, whether or not the other party reciprocates.[78] The peace process undoubtedly climaxed having enhanced the pre-existing relationship between the parties. The PPCC and other consultative bodies ensured that constructive dialogue would be maintained.

- ***Commitments:*** At the conclusion of a negotiation, unless the parties walk away without reaching an agreement, the parties make commitments. Commitments about what each party undertakes to do should be clear, well planned and durable.[79] Unlike early peace agreements, like the one page *Ceasefire Agreement* (1990), the *Bougainville Peace Agreement* was comprehensive and structured to ensure that all parties were clear on their agreed undertakings. Furthermore, compliance with the agreement was not dependent on the cooperation of any absent parties. All of the key players (with the exception of Francis Ona who refused to participate in the peace process), including third parties, were signatories. The commitment was also durable enough to accommodate the resolution of unforseen disputes through mutually acceptable avenues including the PPCC, UNOMB or other peaceful ADR processes.

Through an application of the seven-element problem-solving analysis, the *Bougainville Peace Agreement* can be regarded as a win/win outcome for all concerned. As a testament to its worth, in the almost eight years that have passed since it was signed in August 2001, the agreement has attracted substantial compliance by all parties:

- The last elements of the PNGDF departed Bougainville in April 2003;

- In July 2003 UNOMB verified that Stage II (weapon containment) was complete;

- In December 2003 the PPCC decided that all contained weapons would be destroyed and Stage III (weapon destruction) commenced;

- By May 2004 the UNOMB had verified that Stage III (weapon destruction) was complete and that Bougainville was now stable enough for elections to take place for a BAG; and

- Elections for the BAG were conducted from 20 May to 2 June 2005, resulting in the democratic election of a 39-member BAG on 15 June 2005.[80]

CONCLUSION

It will take the greater part of the coming decade to conclusively determine the success, or otherwise, of the *Bougainville Peace Agreement*. The agreement took almost 13 years to materialise, demonstrating the complexity of intractable violent conflicts, and the significant period required by belligerents to effectively re-establish relationships, communication and to heal deep-seated differences. Notwithstanding initial setbacks, an application of the Harvard Negotiation Project's seven elements indicates that a lasting comprehensive political settlement has been negotiated.

The final negotiated outcome represented a win/win for all sides. Whether the parties knew it or not, this result was gained through the employment of problem-solving negotiation, and its subset, breakthrough negotiation (Ury's 'eighteenth camel')[81] to resolve what at first appeared to be intractable differences. By learning to focus on interests rather than positions, both sides invented a new way to divide the 'orange'[82] and left the negotiating table with grace and, most importantly, their relationship enhanced. The Bougainville experience also reinforces that the many traps and pitfalls, tools and aids commonly identified in conventional negotiations are equally transferable to international dispute resolution scenarios.

The Bougainville Peace Process heralded a revolution in military-political affairs whereby a previously unexplored application for ADR processes was discovered, far removed from a conventional context. To the Australian Defence Force (ADF), at least, ADR demonstrated itself to be a viable alternative to armed intervention in regional disputes. Accordingly, ADF members and their coalition partners, and the negotiations they are facilitating, would stand to benefit from enhanced and comprehensive training in negotiation techniques when confronted by conflict situations comparable to Bougainville. To the Challenges Project:

> negotiation techniques ... should be at the core of all peace operations training. Lower ranks should have a rudimentary understanding, while more senior mission personnel should be proficient. Negotiation techniques improve both civil-military interaction and liaison competencies, and promote cross-culture communication, active listening and conflict management skills.[83]

With Australian and coalition forces currently deployed across the globe on nation-building operations within states torn apart by complex and longstanding internal civil and political unrest, there remains considerable lessons to be learnt from the Bougainville experience and the use of ADR techniques as a viable means of resolving such conflict.

Notes

1 Background information obtained from: R.R.E. Bowd, *Doves Over the Pacific: In Pursuit of Peace and Stability in Bougainville*, Australian Military History Publications, Sydney, 1997, pp. 21–35.
2 Report of the Visit of the Australian Parliamentary Delegation to Bougainville 18–22 April 1994, *Bougainville: A Pacific Solution*, Australian Government Publishing Service, Canberra, 1994.
3 J.W. Burton, *Conflict Resolution: Its Language and Processes* Scarecrow Press, Lanham, MD, 1996, pp. 7–8.
4 Burton, *Conflict Resolution: Its Language and Processes*, p. 7.
5 Burton, *Conflict Resolution: Its Language and Processes*, p. 8.
6 Burton, *Conflict Resolution: Its Language and Processes*, pp. 8–12.
7 H. Astor and C. Chinkin, *Dispute Resolution in Australia* (2nd ed.), LexisNexis Butterworths, Sydney, 2002, p. 166.
8 C. Menkel-Meadow, 'Lawyer Negotiations: Theories and Realities-What we Learn from Mediation' *Modern Law Review*, vol. 56, no. 3, May 1993, p. 367.

9 W. Ury, *Getting Past No: Negotiating With Difficult People* ,Random House, London, 1991, pp. 98–99; and R. Fisher and W. Ury, *Getting to Yes: Negotiating Agreements Without Giving In*, Random House, London, 1992, pp. 49–51.

10 Ury, *Getting to Yes: Negotiating Agreements Without Giving In*, pp. 38–40.

11 R. Fisher and D. Ertel, *Getting Ready To Negotiate: the Getting to Yes Workbook*,: Penguin Books, New York, 1995, p. 21.

12 R. Fisher, *Beyond Machiavelli: Tools for Coping with Conflict*, Penguin Books, New York, 1996, p. 76; and G. Tillett, *Resolving Conflict: A Practical Approach* (2nd ed.), Oxford University Press, Melbourne, 1999), p. 71.

13 Fisher and Ury, *Getting to Yes: Negotiating Agreements Without Giving In*, pp. 104–111.

14 Fisher and Ury, *Getting to Yes: Negotiating Agreements Without Giving In*, p. 51.

15 Ury, *Getting Past No: Negotiating With Difficult People*, pp. 7–9.

16 Ury, *Getting Past No: Negotiating With Difficult People*, p.10. Note that William Ury states that the strategy is so applicable to all disputes that it can even be employed by 'diplomats trying to stave off a war'.

17 A. Regan, *Bougainville: The Peace Process and Beyond*, Submission to the Foreign Affairs Sub- Committee of the Joint Standing Committee on Foreign Affairs, Defence and Trade Inquiry, Canberra, June 1999, p. 23, available at <http://www.aph.gov.au/house/committee/jfadt/bougainville/BVrepindx.htm>, accessed 31 March 2009.

18 D. Oliver, *Black Islanders: A Personal Perspective of Bougainville 1937–1991* ,Hyland House, Melbourne, 1991, p. 251.

19 Regan, *Bougainville: The Peace Process and Beyond*, p. 21.

20 R.J. Lewicki, D.M. Saunders, J.M. Minton and B. Barry, *Negotiation: Readings. Exercises and Cases* (4th ed.), McGraw-Hill, New York, 2003, p. 439.

21 Lewicki, Saunders, Minton and Barry, *Negotiation: Readings. Exercises and Cases* (4th ed.), p. 437.

22 E.P. Wolfers, *International Peace Missions In Bougainville, Papua New Guinea, 1990–2005: Host State Perceptions*, Regional Forum on Reinventing Government Exchange and Transfer of Innovations for Transparent Governance and State Capacity, Nadi, 20–22 February 2006, p. 10.

23 Tillett, *Resolving Conflict: A Practical Approach* (2nd ed.), pp. 45–46.

24 Tillett, *Resolving Conflict: A Practical Approach* (2nd ed.), pp. 45–51.

25 National Alternative Dispute Resolution Advisory Council, *Alternative Dispute Resolution Definitions,* NADRAC, Canberra, 1997, p. 8.

26 Astor and Chinkin, *Dispute Resolution in Australia*, 2nd ed., p. 88.

27 Astor and Chinkin, *Dispute Resolution in Australia*, 2nd ed., p. 88.

28 B.S. Mayer, *Beyond Neutrality: Confronting the Crisis in Conflict Resolution*, Jossey-Bass, San Francisco, 2004, p. 84.

29 M. Brandon and L. Robertson, *Conflict and Dispute Resolution: A Guide for Practice*, Oxford University Press, Melbourne, 2007, p. 195.

30 L. Nathan, 'Undue Pressure: International Mediation in Africa Civil Wars', in L. Reychler and T. Paffenholz, *Peace Building: A Field Guide*, Lynne Rienner, Boulder, CO, 2001, p. 185.

31 W.P. Smith, 'Effectiveness of the Biased Mediator', *Negotiation Journal*, vol. 1, no. 4, 2 July 2007, pp. 363.

32 Nathan, 'Undue Pressure: International Mediation in Africa Civil Wars', p. 185.

33 Nathan, 'Undue Pressure: International Mediation in Africa Civil Wars', pp. 185–86.

34 The Challenges Project, *Challenges of Peace Operations: Into the 21st Century—Concluding Report: 1997–2002*, Elanders Gotab, Stockholm, 2002, pp. 269–70.

35 Brandon and Robertson, *Conflict and Dispute Resolution: A Guide for Practice,* p. 195.

36 Fisher, *Beyond Machiavelli: Tools for Coping with Conflict*, pp. 96–98.

37 Tillett, *Resolving Conflict: A Practical Approach* (2nd ed.), p. 68.

38 A.J. Regan, 'Phases in the Negotiation Process', in A. Carl and L. Garasu (eds), *Weaving Consensus: The Papua New Guinea—Bougainville peace process* (Accord issue 12, 2002), available at <http://www.c-r.org/our-work/accord/pngbougainville/phases.php>, accessed 31 March 2009.

39 J. Bercovitch, 'International Mediation and Intractable Conflict', January 2004, available at <http://www.beyondintractability.org/essay/med_intractable_conflict/>, accessed 25 March 2009

40 G. Hassall, 'Peace Agreements in the Pacific Islands', in *Regional Workshop on Conflict Prevention and Peacebuilding in the Pacific*, Pacific Islands Forum Secretariat, United Nations Department of Political Affairs, Nadi, 25–27 April 2005, p. 3.

41 Regan, *Bougainville: The Peace Process and Beyond*, p. 22.

42 M. Miriori, 'A Bougainville Interim Government (BIG) Perspective on Early Peace Efforts', in Carl and Garasu (eds), *Weaving Consensus: The Papua New Guinea—Bougainville peace process,* (Accord issue 12, 2002), available at <http://www.c-r.org/our-work/accord/png-bougainville/big-perspective.php>, accessed 31 March 2009.

43 P. Sohia, 'Early Interventions', in. Carl and Garasu (eds), *Weaving Consensus: The Papua New Guinea—Bougainville peace process.* (Accord issue 12, 2002), available at <http://www.c-r.org/our-work/accord/png-bougainville/early-interventions.php>, accessed 31 March 2009,

44 Miriori, 'A Bougainville Interim Government (BIG) Perspective on Early Peace Efforts'.

45 The Challenges Project, *Challenges of Peace Operations*, p. 115.

46 Bercovitch, 'International Mediation and Intractable Conflict'.

47 Tillett, *Resolving Conflict: A Practical Approach* (2nd ed.), p. 77.

48 The Challenges Project, *Challenges of Peace Operations*, p. 270.

49 Fisher, *Beyond Machiavelli: Tools for Coping with Conflict*, pp. 23–24.

50 Astor and Chinkin, *Dispute Resolution in Australia* (2nd ed.), p. 114.

51 The Challenges Project, *Challenges of Peace Operations*, p. 119.

52 J. Emmerig, 'Advanced Negotiation for Lawyers: Tricks and Traps in Negotiation' August 2005 (unpublished), p. 11; and Hassall, 'Peace Agreements in the Pacific Islands', p. 14.

53 Fisher and Ertel, *Getting Ready To Negotiate: the Getting to Yes Workbook*, p. 96.

54 Emmerig, 'Advanced Negotiation for Lawyers: Tricks and Traps in Negotiation', p. 7.

55 Regan, 'Phases in the Negotiation Process'.

56 Fisher, *Beyond Machiavelli: Tools for Coping with Conflict*, p. 76.

57 R. Tapi, 'From Burnham to Buin: Sowing the Seeds of Peace in the Land of the Snow Capped Mountains', in Carl and Garasu (eds), *Weaving Consensus: The Papua New Guinea—Bougainville peace process* (Accord issue 12, 2002),available at <http://www.c-r.org/our-work/accord/png-bougainville/burnham-buin.php>, accessed 25 March 2009.

58 Tillett, *Resolving Conflict: A Practical Approach* (2nd ed.), p. 52.

59 Tapi, 'From Burnham to Buin: Sowing the Seeds of Peace in the Land of the Snow Capped Mountains'.

60 Ury, *Getting Past No: Negotiating With Difficult People*, p. 42; Fisher and Ertel, *Getting Ready To Negotiate: the Getting to Yes Workbook*, pp. 86–88; and Fisher, *Beyond Machiavelli: Tools for Coping with Conflict*, pp. 78–79.

61 A. Limbury, 'Principled Negotiation and Constructive Mediation', Seminar Paper: 'Negotiation Skills for Lawyers', Centre for Continuing Education, Faculty of Law, University of New South Wales, 4 August 2005, p. 9.

62 Limbury, 'Principled Negotiation and Constructive Mediation', pp. 9–10.

63 Interestingly, in traditional islander culture, emotions are acknowledged as key to the successful resolution of disputes. Negotiations are traditionally followed by a 'sing sing' (also known as a reconciliation ceremony), whereby opposing parties publically acknowledge the agreement reached and forgive past wrongs.

64 Tapi, 'From Burnham to Buin: Sowing the Seeds of Peace in the Land of the Snow Capped Mountains'; and Burnham II Preparatory Talks, Burnham Military Camp, New Zealand, 1–10 October 1997, *Record of Understanding* (dated 10 October 1997).

65 J. Eagles, 'Aid as an Instrument for Peace: A Civil Society Perspective', in Carl and Garasu (eds), *Weaving Consensus: The Papua New Guinea—Bougainville peace process* (Accord issue 12, 2002), available at <http://www.c-r.org/our-work/accord/png-bougainville/aid.php>, accessed 31 March 2009; Regan, *Bougainville: The Peace Process and Beyond*, p. 21; and Hassall, 'Peace Agreements in the Pacific Islands', p. 13.

66 Hassall, 'Peace Agreements in the Pacific Islands', p. 14.

67 Ury, *Getting Past No: Negotiating With Difficult People*, pp. 113–14.

68 K. Patterson, 'Australia Promotes Gender Equality and Peace-Building' in *Focus*, Canberra, March 2001, available at , a <http://www.womenwarpeace.org/webfm_send/92>, accessed 31 March 2009.

69 See also R. Saovana-Spriggs, 'Bougainville Women's Role in Conflict Resolution in the Bougainville Peace Process', in S. Dinnen, A. Jowitt and T. Newton (eds), *A Kind of Mending: Restorative Justice in the Pacific Islands*, Pandanus Books, Canberra, 2003, pp. 195–214.

70 Ury, *Getting Past No: Negotiating With Difficult People*, pp. 7–9.

71 Fisher and Ertel, *Getting Ready To Negotiate: the Getting to Yes Workbook*, p. 21; and Fisher, *Beyond Machiavelli: Tools for Coping with Conflict*, pp. 74–76.

72 Fisher and Ertel, *Getting Ready To Negotiate: the Getting to Yes Workbook*, p. 33; and R. Fisher, *Beyond Machiavelli: Tools for Coping with Conflict*, pp. 76–77.

73 Fisher, *Beyond Machiavelli: Tools for Coping with Conflict*, pp. 96–98.

74 Fisher and Ertel, *Getting Ready To Negotiate: the Getting to Yes Workbook*, pp. 45–48; and Fisher, *Beyond Machiavelli: Tools for Coping with Conflict*, pp. 77–78.

75 Fisher and Ertel, *Getting Ready To Negotiate: the Getting to Yes Workbook*, pp. 61–64; and Fisher, *Beyond Machiavelli: Tools for Coping with Conflict*, p. 77.

76 UN support for various cease-fire agreements on Bougainville also carried a great deal of legitimacy. Refer also R. Fisher, *Basic Negotiating Strategy: International Conflict for Beginners*, Penguin Press, London, 1971, p. 142.

77 Fisher and Ertel, *Getting Ready To Negotiate: the Getting to Yes Workbook*, pp. 76–78; and Fisher, *Beyond Machiavelli: Tools for Coping with Conflict*, pp. 80–81.

78 Fisher and Ertel, *Getting Ready To Negotiate: the Getting to Yes Workbook*, pp. 86–88; and Fisher, *Beyond Machiavelli: Tools for Coping with Conflict*, pp. 78–79.

79 Fisher and Ertel, *Getting Ready To Negotiate: the Getting to Yes Workbook*, pp. 96–99; and Fisher, *Beyond Machiavelli: Tools for Coping with Conflict*, pp. 81–82.

80 Historical information sourced from R.R.E. Bowd, *Doves Over the Pacific: In Pursuit of Peace and Stability in Bougainville*, pp. 134–48.

81 A parable used by William Ury whereby the only way to equally divide an inheritance of 17 camels by two, three and nine (one half to the eldest son, one third to the middle son, and one ninth to the youngest son) was through an outsider providing an 'eighteenth' camel. Eighteen could be divided equally between the three sons (nine camels to the eldest son, six to the middle son and two to the youngest son) (making 17 camels equally divisible). The one camel remaining was returned to the third-party. Ury, *Getting Past No: Negotiating With Difficult People*, pp. 137–38.

82 Roger Fisher and William Ury tell the story of two sisters quarrelling over an orange to typify how many people negotiate. The two sisters arrive at the natural decision to cut the orange in two. Following this, one sister ate the fruit and threw away the peel and the other threw away the fruit and used the peel from her half to bake a cake. 'Too many negotiations end up with half an orange for each side instead of the whole fruit for one and the whole peel for the other'. Fisher and Ury, *Getting to Yes: Negotiating Agreements Without Giving In*, p. 59.

83 The Challenges Project, *Challenges of Peace Operations*, p. 239.

Appendix

In Search of a Comprehensive Negotiated Agreement to the Bougainville 'Crisis': 1988–2001

Ser.	Period of Negoti-ation	Date of Agreement	Place of Agreement	Title of Agreement	Agreement	The Parties Key PNG Government/ Pro-PNG Government representatives	Leader—Bougainville Delegation	Chairperson/ Mediator/ Facilitator	3rd Party Involvement (Witnesses and Observers)	Post Agreement Events
1	Dec 1988	8 Dec 1988	Arovo Island, Bougainville	Memorandum of Understanding (MOU)	• National Government to address the issue of improving community services	Akoka Doi (Deputy Prime Minister and leader of the Special Committee on Bougainville)	Francis Ona (leader of the New Panguna Landowners Association and BRA)			• 1 April 1972: Panguna Mine commences operations • 1 September 1975: Bougainville (unlawfully) declares independence as the Republic of North Solomons (fails to attract international support). PNG legislation passes giving Bougainville greater autonomy as a compromise • 16 September 1975: PNG becomes an independent state • 1976: North Solomons Provincial Government established • 1979: Panguna Landowners Association (PLA) is formed to represent landowner interests • August 1987: New Panguna Landowners Association (NPLA) appears and challenges legitimacy of the PLA (Francis Ona, an employee of the Panguna Mine, is its Secretary) • 4 July 1998: Rabbie Namaliu replaces Paias Wingti as PM of PNG • November 1988: Commencement of highly organised arson attacks by NPLA leader Francis Ona in Panguna area. Militants become known as the Bougainville Revolutionary Army (BRA) • 18 April 1989: Francis Ona contacts the NSPG and advises that secession, as opposed to compensation, is the main issue • 8 December 1989: On the night the MOU is signed police arrest key landowners leading to the agreement being renounced by the BRA leadership • April 1989: Francis Ona declares that secession is the organisation's main objective
2	2 May–Oct 1989	12 Sept 1989 (intended date of meeting)	Arawa, Bougainville	Bika Report	• Proposed package between the North Solomons Provincial Government (NSPG) and National Government • Major public works favoring landowners affected by the mine • Equity in BCL and generous financial concessions • (Note: Meeting never took place, Ona demanded that secession must be discussed and John Bika was assassinated on 10 September 1989)	National Government		NSPG **(attempting to facilitate between the BRA and National Government)**		• 15 May 1989: Panguna Mine is forced to close • Mid-1989: Australia donates four Iroquois helicopters to the PNGDF (subsequently employed in Bougainville for offensive operations (as gunships) in contravention of agreed conditions (the helicopters were only to be used for transportation, surveillance and medical evacuation activities). A 1991 Parliamentary Committee concluded that the donation was the most publicised and controversial action of the Australian government at a crucial stage in the Bougainville crisis • 26 June 1989: State of Emergency declared • 12 September 1989: Assassination of Provincial Minister John Bika prompts the PNG Government to intensify efforts to find a military solution to the Crisis • 1989: PNGDF Operation FOOTLOOSE in the Kongara

Ser.	Period of Negotia-tion	Date of Agreement	Place of Agreement	Title of Agreement	Agreement	The Parties Key PNG Government/ Pro-PNG Government representatives	Leader—Bougainville Delegation	Chairperson/ Mediator/ Facilitator	3rd Party Involvement (Witnesses and Observers)	Post Agreement Events
3	Oct 1989	27 Oct 1989	Arawa, Bougainville	Namaliu Agreement and Peace Ceremony	• All parties (except Francis Ona) (except Francis Ona and the BRA) commit to cease hostilities and restore law and order	• Rabbie Namaliu (Prime Minister of PNG) • Joseph Kabui (Premier of the North Solomons Provincial Government) • Chairman and Manager of BCL • Church Leaders • Traditional Leaders				BRA refuses to participate and militant activities intensify
4	Jan–Mar 1990	1 Mar 1990	Arawa, Bougainville	Agreement to End Hostilities on Bougainville (Bougainville Ceasefire Agreement)	• Ceasefire from 2 March 1990 • Total withdrawal of PNG Security Forces by 16 March 1990 • BRA disarmament under supervision of International Observer Group (IOG) • Create conditions for face-to-face dialogue between the disputants	Colonel Neo Nuia (Deputy Controller of the State of Emergency)	Sam Kauona (BRA Military Commander)	Professor Peter Wallensteen (Uppsala University, Sweden) **(Facilitator)**	Facilitated by the Commonwealth Secretariat, London: IOG of 11 members from Ghana, Trinidad, Nigeria, Britain, Canada, Sweden and the Netherlands	• 14 February 1990: Valentine's Day Massacre. The PNGDF tortures, kills and throws suspected rebels from Australian donated helicopters. Houses are burned in the Kieta district (Note: this was just one of numerous atrocities on both sides of the conflict) • 12 March 1990: All PNG Security Forces are withdrawn from Bougainville • 12–16 March 1990: IOG led by the Commonwealth Secretariat (Ghana, Trinidad, Nigeria, Britain, Canada, Sweden and the Netherlands) deploys to Bougainville and reports that all parties have complied with their undertakings • March 1990: BRA repudiates agreement and takes control of the island • March 1990 (onwards): BRA/BIG proves incapable of maintaining law and order and criminal gangs and factions form • April 1990: BRA establishes a political arm, the Bougainville Interim Government (BIG) and declares it the legitimate authority on Bougainville • 2 May 1990: PNG declares a total blockade on Bougainville • 17 May 1990: Francis Ona makes a unilateral declaration of Bougainville independence • May 1990: Leaders of Nissan (Green) Island invite a return of the PNGDF and pro-PNGDF anti-BRA Bougainville Resistance Forces (BRF) emerge to protect villages from the BRA and increasingly lawlessness
5	29 Jul–5 Aug 1990	5 Aug 1990	HMNZS *Endeavour*, Kieta, Bougainville	Endeavour Accord	• Long term political status of Bougainville would be addressed as part of future talks • End the Blockade on services and supplies to Bougainville • Conduct further talks within eight weeks	Michael Somare (PNG Foreign Minister, 'Father of the Nation' and former Prime Minister)	Joseph Kabui (BIG Minister for Peace, Justice and Police and former Premier of the North Solomons Provincial Government (NSPG)		• Government of New Zealand • International Observers (New Zealand, Canada and Vanuatu) • Royal New Zealand Navy (RNZN)(Task Group comprising the naval supply vessel HMNZS *Endeavour* and the frigates HMNZS *Waikato* and HMNZS *Wellington*)	• 27 July–6 August 1990: New Zealand Navy Task Group deploys to Bougainville in support of peace talks • August 1990–February 1991: PNG Government loses interest in agreement and BRA refuses to allow aid to arrive—Blockade continues • 29 August 1990: NSPG suspended and an provincial administration in exile is established at Rabaul • September 1990: Fighting breaks out on Buka between local BRA and BRA factions—the PNGDF is invited to return to the island to re-establish law and order
6	5 Oct 1990	5 Oct 1990	Buka, Bougainville	Malagan Accord (Kavieng Agreement)	• Return of government services to Buka • Return of the PNGDF to Buka	Government Officials	Leaders of Buka Island			

Ser.	Period of Negotiation	Date of Agreement	Place of Agreement	Title of Agreement	Agreement	The Parties Key PNG Government/ Pro-PNG Government representatives	Leader—Bougainville Delegation	Chairperson/ Mediator/ Facilitator	3rd Party Involvement (Witnesses and Observers)	Post Agreement Events
7	22–23 Jan 1991	23 Jan 1991	Honiara, Solomon Islands	Honiara Declaration on Peace, Reconciliation and Rehabilitation on Bougainville	• Annul the unilateral declaration of independence made by Francis Ona on 17 May 1990 • Restoration of essential services • Promise of amnesty for the BRA • Introduction of a Multinational Supervisory Team (MST) to oversee disarmament • Review the agreement every six months	Michael Somare (PNG Foreign Minister, 'Father of the Nation' and former Prime Minister)	Joseph Kabui (BIG Minister for Peace, Justice and Police and former Premier of the North Solomons Provincial Government (NSPG))	Bishop Lesley Beseto (Chairman of SICA) **(Mediator)**	• Solomon Islands Government • Solomon Islands Christian Association (SICA)	• Unilateral declaration is annulled • BRA hardliners immediately repudiate the Honiara Declaration and refuse to disarm • PNGDF fails to deploy a MST and only selectively restores services to PNGDF controlled areas
8	7–8 Sept 1991	No agreement	MV Kris	Agenda setting talks for reviewing the Honiara Declaration	• Finalise agenda for review of the Honiara • Declaration (Note: no subsequent talks ever took place)	Brown Bai (Chairman of the PNG National Security Advisory Committee)	Martin Miriori (BIG Secretary)			• December 1991: PNG National Government installs Interim Legal Authorities in PNGDF controlled areas • 1992: BIG establishes a Bougainville Interim Peace Office in Honiara, Solomon Islands under Martin Miriori • 17 July 1992: Paias Wingti replaces Rabbie Namaliu as PM of PNG • 1991-1994: Large scale PNGDF military operations on Bougainville to regain control of areas north of Wakunai and large parts of southwest Bougainville including Buin and Arawa • April 1993: Week long pan-Bougainville Leaders' Forum held in Buka (BIG/BRA, local leaders and other locally affected parties). Resolutions included abandoning secession, reinstatement of the NSPG and peace talks with the BRA in the absence of the PNG Government
9	4–5 June 1994; 10–11 June 1994	11 June 1994	Honiara, Solomon Islands	Tambea Talks	• Initial agenda setting for Ministerial level dialogue • Reaffirm commitment to the peace process	Senior Government Officials	Sam Kauona (BRA Military Commander – representing BIG/BRA)		Facilitated by the Solomon Islands Government	August 1994: PNGDF initiates Operation HIGH SPEED I, a costly military effort to retake the Panguna Mine
10	26–27 Aug 1994	27 Aug 1994	Tambea, Solomon Islands	Tambea Record	• Set agenda for Honiara Talks • Continuing consultative process (four stages): - Stage I: Consultative meeting between the Deputy Prime Minister and Sam Kauona on 23 August 1994 - Stage II: High Level Consultative meeting between PNG Senior officials and the Commander of the BRA and the representatives of the organisation known as the Bougainville Interim Government - Stage III: Ministerial meeting to be held on 2nd September in Solomon Islands - Stage IV: The Bougainville Peace Conference to be held in Bougainville	Brown Bai (Secretary to the Department of Prime Minister and Cabinet, Prime Minister's Office)	Sam Kauona (BRA Military Commander — representing BIG/BRA)	Francis Saemala (Deputy Prime Minister and Minister for Foreign Affairs of Solomon Islands) **(Convener and Chair-person)**	Facilitated by the Solomon Islands Government	30 August 1994: Julius Chan replaces Paias Wingti as PNG PM and places Bougainville at the top of his priorities

Ser.	Period of Negotiation	Date of Agreement	Place of Agreement	Title of Agreement	Agreement	The Parties Key PNG Government/ Pro-PNG Government representatives	Leader—Bougainville Delegation	Chairperson/ Mediator/ Facilitator	3rd Party Involvement (Witnesses and Observers)	Post Agreement Events
11	2–3 Sept 1994	3 Sept 1994	Honiara, Solomon Islands	Honiara Commitments to Peace on Bougainville	• Immediate declaration of Peace • Forces to remain in static positions • Deployment of South Pacific Peace-Keeping Force (SPPKF) as soon as practicably possible after a ceasefire declaration • Arawa Peace Conference convened no later than 10 October 1994	Julius Chan (Prime Minister of PNG)	Sam Kauona (BRA Military Commander — representing BIG/BRA)	Francis Billy Hilly (Prime Minister of Solomon Islands) **(Convener and Chairperson)**	Facilitated by the Solomon Islands Government	Unfortunately, Sam Kauona (BRA) did not return to Bougainville to brief the BRA on the agreement and this was to have unfortunate consequences
12	4–8 Sept 1994	8 Sept 1994	Honiara, Solomon Islands	Ceasefire Agreement (and Implementation Instrument)	• Ceasefire to take effect midnight 9 September 1994 • SPPKF invited to Bougainville to monitor ceasefire and facilitate Arawa Peace Conference • Establishment of Neutral Zones during Arawa Peace Conference • SPPKF will enter Bougainville at least 7 days prior to the Conference and carry out its functions for at least 14 days • Security of neutral SPPKF is guaranteed	• LTCOL Davey Ugul (Director Land Operations, PNGDF) • Gabriel Dusava (Secretary, Department of Foreign Affairs and Trade, PNG)	• Sam Kauona (BRA Military Commander) • Martin Miriori (Representing the organisation known as BIG)		Facilitated by: • Solomon Islands Government Witnessed by: • Frederick Soaki (Police Commissioner, Solomon Islands) • Thomas Anis (Chairman, Bougainville Interim Authorities, PNG)	• 23 September 1994: Julius Chan concedes to BRA insistence that the UN endorse the SPPKF deployment and seeks formal UN recognition • 27 September 1994: UN Secretary-General Boutros Boutros-Gali is briefed on the Bougainville situation • 6 October 1994: Boutros Boutros-Gali writes to Julius Chan and formally endorses the peace process. The UN indicates its willingness to assist by providing joint secretarial services and a Japanese Political Observer, Hiko Miramura to the BPC • 4–20 October 1994: SPPKF and supporting logistical assets including HMAS *Tobruk* and HMAS *Manoora* deploy to Bougainville via Honiara to support BPC • 7 October 1994: Chan temporarily lifts blockade on Bougainville to allow for SPPKF deployment
13	10–14 Oct 1994	14 Oct 1994	Arawa, Bougainville	Bougainville Peace Conference (no formal agreement reached)	It was agreed that, despite the failure of the Conference, talks would continue to seek to resolve the conflict. The official agenda was to discuss: • Continuation of peace • Pardon, amnesty and temporary refuge • Restoration and reconstruction of essential services • Reconciliation and compensation • Discussions on political future of Bougainville would be deferred (secession was not on the agenda although PNG Officials conceded that this should be the focus of subsequent talks in the presence of the BIG/BRA) The BRA/BIG Hijacked talks by tabling three demands: • An indefinite mandate for the SPPKF • Total withdrawal of the PNGDF • Indefinite duration for the BPC	Julius Chan (Prime Minister of PNG opened the Conference). In permanent attendance were high level Officials	Temporary representation by Ishmael Toroama (BRA Acting Commander and Chief of Staff, leader Kongara Region)	George Lepping (former Governor-General of the Solomon Islands) **(Chairperson)**	• Solomon Islands Government • Government of Australia • Government of New Zealand • Government of Fiji • Government of Tonga • Government of Vanuatu • UN Political Observer	• BIG/BRA leadership refused to attend but were represented on occasion by Ishmael Toroama • 13 October 1994: Toroama brings the BPC to an end when he announces BRA demands of total withdrawal of the PNGDF, secession from PNG and an indefinite mandate for the SPPKF and BPC. PM Julius Chan cancel's the 'sing sing' ceremony scheduled to be conducted at the conclusion of the BPC with foreign dignitaries and officials invited October 1994: Several reasons, many quite valid, were given for the BRA non-attendance at the BPC
14	17–18 Oct 1994	18 Oct 1994	Arawa, Bougainville	North Nasoi Agreement	• Acknowledged the principles and matters of concerns recognised by the parties • Continuation of the Ceasefire Agreement and peace process • Shared blame between the parties	PNG National Government Officials and Commander PNGDF, Brigadier-General Tony Huai	BIG/BRA splinter factions (including BRA Commanders of the North Nasioi Area			

Ser.	Period of Negotiation	Date of Agreement	Place of Agreement	Title of Agreement	Agreement	The Parties Key PNG Government/ Pro-PNG Government representatives	Leader—Bougainville Delegation	Chairperson/ Mediator/ Facilitator	3rd Party Involvement (Witnesses and Observers)	Post Agreement Events
					• The Village Council of Chiefs and BRA Commanders who signed the agreement accepted Theodore Miriung as Interim Chairman of the North Nasioi Village Council of Chiefs		who were frustrated with hardliners) (13 pages of signatories)			
15	25 Nov 1994	25 Nov 1994	Waigani, Bougainville	Charter of Mirigini	• Commitment to peace process • Step up the pace and momentum of bringing normalcy, services and legal authority to Bougainville • By March 1995 the National Government would establish a Bougainville Transitional Government (BTG) to replace the NSPG • Commitment to an active program of consultations and negotiations on a political settlement • Maintain dialogue on other issues pertinent to resolution of the crisis including reconciliation, reconstruction and restoration of services	• Julius Chan (Prime Minister of PNG) • Chairman of respective Interim Authorities				10 April 1995: Bougainville Transitional Government (BTG) is established at Buka. Theodore Miriung is elected Premier
16	18 May–3 Aug 1995	18 May 1995	Port Moresby, PNG	Waigani Communiqué	• BTG established • Commitment to ongoing programs for consultations and negotiations on all issues pertinent to the resolution of the Bougainville situation (Pardon Amnesty and Temporary Refuge; Reconciliation and Compensation; Restoration of Services and Reconstruction of Bougainville; and others)	• Julius Chan (Prime Minister of PNG) • Theodore Miriung (Premier of the BTG)				
17		29 July 1995	Port Moresby, PNG	Joint Statement on Amnesty						
18		3 Aug 1995	Port Moresby, PNG	Areas of Common Understanding	• Amnesty for those who have committed crimes during the Bougainville conflict • Arms amnesty • Commitment to a "new projects" approach for all new developmental projects in the province • Proposed policy on the future of armed youth, their disarmament and rehabilitation • Future political status of Bougainville • Parallel negotiations should commence between the BTG and the BIG/BRA					

Ser.	Period of Negotiation	Date of Agreement	Place of Agreement	Title of Agreement	Agreement	The Parties Key PNG Government/ Pro-PNG Government representatives	Leader—Bougainville Delegation	Chairperson/ Mediator/ Facilitator	3rd Party Involvement (Witnesses and Observers)	Post Agreement Events
19	9–12 Sept 1995	12 Sept 1995	Cairns, Australia	Joint Press Statement (Preliminary Talks—CAIRNS I)	• Identify problems • Address areas of common understanding • Lay groundwork for an all-inclusive meeting of Bougainville leaders	Theodore Miriung (Premier of the BTG)	Martin Miriori (BIG Secretary)		Facilitated by the Government of Australia	
20	14–18 Dec 1995	18 Dec 1995	Cairns, Australia	Joint Communiqué (CAIRNS II—All Bougainville Leaders Talks)	• Cessation of violence and security issues • Future status of Bougainville • Confidence Building • Human rights matters • Renewal and socio-economic development • Procedural issues and calendar	• Theodore Miriung (Premier of the BTG) • Michael Laimo, MP (Member for South Bougainville was also a signatory on the Communiqué	• Joseph Kabui (BIG Minister for Peace, Justice and Police and former Premier of the North Solomons Provincial Government (NSPG)) • Sam Kauona (BRA Military Commander)	• Professor Francisco Vendrell (UN Director of the Asia Pacific Political Division) • Dr Kris Srinivasan (Deputy Secretary-General of the Common-wealth Secretariat) **(Co- Chair-persons)**	• Government of Australia Observers: • International Commission of Jurists (NGO) • Moral Rearmament (NGO) • Secretary General of Unrepresented Nations Peoples Organization (NGO)	• 3 January 1996: BRA/BIG Delegation led by Joseph Kabui was attacked by the PNGDF at the sea border between Bougainville and the Solomon Islands • 11 March 1996: John Howard becomes PM of Australia and his new Government calls for a change of policy toward the management of the Bougainville Crisis. Alexander Downer becomes Australia's Foreign Affairs Minister • 21 March 1996: Following a spate of violence on Bougainville, PNG PM Julius Chan lifts the 'tentative' ceasefire that had been in place since September 1994 and bans official contact between the PNG Government and BIG/BRA • 30 April 1996: UNHCR evacuates Martin Miriori (BIG Secretary) and his family from the Solomon Islands to Amsterdam. Relations between PNG and Solomon Islands improve
21	4 June 1996	4 June 1996	Port Moresby, PNG	Memorandum of Understanding	• Maintain the process of peace, reconciliation and reconstruction on Bougainville, including the impetus created to date • Current term of the BTG be extended beyond the 1997 National Elections • Deliberate further on the level and scope of autonomy for Bougainville • Establish a system of local level government	• Julius Chan (Prime Minister of PNG) • Theodore Miriung (Premier of the BTG)			Government of New Zealand	• May–June 1996: PNGDF commences Operation HIGH SPEED II against the rebels • September 1996: Kangu Beach Massacre. BRA attacks PNGDF stronghold at Kangu and takes 5 PNGDF prisoners • 12 October 1996: Theodore Miriung (BTG Premier and senior negotiator is assassinated at his home in Southern Bougainville. The BRF and PNGDF are implicated • 31 January 1997: The PNG Government signs the 'Sandline Agreement' with international mercenaries • 22 February 1997: 'Sandline Agreement' becomes public • 27 March 1997: Australian Defence Force intercepts and confiscates arms and equipment bound for PNG on an Antinov chartered aircraft • March 1997: PNGDF Commander, Brigadier-General Jerry Singirok calls for the PNG PM Julius Chan to stand down Singirok is subsequently sacked by Julius Chan • 26 March 1997: Julius Chan stands down as PNG PM pending July 1997 elections • April–May 1997: Confidential discussions between BTG and BIG/BRA. Don McKinnon contacts Martin Miriori and conveys New Zealand's proposals for renewed peace efforts in Bougainville • 10–20 June 1997: Solomon Islands Government holds confidential talks with BIG/BRA leaders including Joseph Kabui and Sam Kauona in Honiara, Solomon Islands which furthered the agreement with the BTG to hold talks in Burnham in July 1997 • June 1997: PNG Nationals arrive unexpectedly in Honiara, Solomon Islands prompting fears that the men (claiming to be bricklayers) had been sent as a hit-squad to assassinate the BRA leadership. It later turned out that the men were in Honiara for 'bona fide purposes' • June–July 1997: Australian lawyers, Leo White and Mark Plunkett, run a negotiation course on negotiating skills (and conflict resolution) for parties to the Bougainville Conflict (BTG in Buka and BIG/BRA in Honiara)

Ser.	Period of Negotiation	Date of Agreement	Place of Agreement	Title of Agreement	Agreement	The Parties Key PNG Government/ Pro-PNG Government representatives	Leader—Bougainville Delegation	Chairperson/ Mediator/ Facilitator	3rd Party Involvement (Witnesses and Observers)	Post Agreement Events
22	15–18 June 1997	18 June 1997	Novotel Hotel, Auckland, New Zealand	Confidential talks between BIG/BRA and BTG Buka leaders	Agreement to work toward a Burnham peace process. Before that could occur Bougainvilleans must meet and attempt to resolve their problems. The next stage would involve negotiations with the PNG Government	BTG Buka leaders	BIG/BRA Leaders including Martin Miriori (BIG Secretary)	• Don McKinnon (NZ Foreign Minister) • John Hayes, Bede Corry and Neil Walter (Senior NZ Foreign Ministry Officials) **(Party to the talks)**	Government of New Zealand	June 1988: Bipartisan/National Approach to the crisis shown through the appointment of a Special State Negotiator (Sir John Kaputin) and later the Bipartisan National Committee on Bougainville
23	5–18 July 1997	18 July 1997	Burnham Military Camp, New Zealand	Burnham Declaration (BURNHAM I)	• Establishment of a clear process for the achievement of a political settlement to the war on Bougainville • Commitment to unity and reconciliation at all levels • Establishment of a process for negotiations between Bougainville Leaders and the Government of Papua New Guinea • End to the war and Declaration of Ceasefire to take effect simultaneously with the arrival of the first contingent of the peacekeeping force on Bougainville • Neutral Peacekeeping Force is invited to Bougainville at the beginning of the process for a period of not more than three years, under the auspices of the UN • Any 'Status of Forces' Agreement is agreed to by the State of Papua New Guinea and countries contributing to the Peacekeeping Force, that the Bougainville Interim Government and the Bougainville Transitional Government be fully consulted and be party to it • Demilitarisation of Bougainville—complete withdrawal of the PNGDF within a time frame to be agreed to between Bougainville Leaders and the PNG Government • Laying down of arms by all Bougainvilleans under supervision of the Peacekeeping Force	Gerard Sinato (Premier BTG)	Joseph Kabui (leader of BIG/BRA delegation)	• Martin Miriori (BIG Secretary) • Commissioner Simon Pentanu (PNG Chief Ombudsman) —also a Bougainvillean (Co-Chairpersons)	Facilitated and observed by: • Government of New Zealand Observed by: • Don McKinnon (NZ Foreign Minister) • John Hayes, Bede Corry and Neil Walter (Senior NZ Foreign Ministry Officials)	• 1997: Francis Ona objects to the direction of the Peace Process and instead forms a self-proclaimed Me'ekamui Government and Me'ekamui Defence Force (MDF) (the dominant force in the MDF is the BRA 'A' Company). Ona continues to refuse to participate in the peace process and declares a 15km 'No Go Zone' around MDF strongholds vicinity Panguna and Tonu. The disputants, and the TMG/PMG respect the 'No Go Zone' • 22 July 1997: Bill Skate replaces Julius Chan as PM of PNG following his defeat at the polls • July 1997: As a goodwill gesture post-Burnham 1, the BRA agreed to release five PNGDF soldiers captured during a BRA attach on the PNGDF outpost at Kangu Beach, Southern Bougainville in September 1996. In return, the PNGDF guaranteed the delegation safe passage back to Bougainville • August 1997: Australian Foreign Minister, Alexander Downer, reverses Australia's long standing policy of no ministerial or official contact with the BRA by meeting with Moses Havini (BIG) in Sydney. Alexander Downer subsequently announced increased Australian aid for Bougainville reconstruction (A$100 million over five years)

Ser.	Period of Negotia-tion	Date of Agreement	Place of Agreement	Title of Agreement	Agreement	The Parties Key PNG Government/ Pro-PNG Government representatives	Leader—Bougainville Delegation	Chairperson/ Mediator/ Facilitator	3rd Party Involvement (Witnesses and Observers)	Post Agreement Events
					• Lifting of Blockade and Removal of Restrictions—need for access throughout Bougainville to relevant donor organisations and other humanitarian agencies, including ICRC and UNICEF, for the implementation of health and education programs, and for the restoration of basic needs • Political Process—people of Bougainville, as a people, freely and democratically exercise their right to determine their political future • Commencement of Process and Venue for First Meeting—first meeting of Bougainville Leaders with the Government of Papua New Guinea no later than September 1997 in a neutral place outside Papua New Guinea or Bougainville					
24	1–10 Oct 1997	10 Oct 1997	Burnham Military Camp, New Zealand	Burnham Truce (BURNHAM II)	• Leaders affirmed objectives of BURNHAM I • Leaders agreed to meet on a regular basis to monitor the implementation of the commitment • Leaders agreed to invite a neutral regional Truce Monitoring Group (TMG) to monitor the terms of the truce	• Robert Igara (Secretary for Prime Minister) • Kapeatu Puaria (BTG Legal Advisor) Witnessed by: • BRF Leaders, PNGDF Representatives, PNGD leaders, PNG Security Force leaders	• Martin Miriori (BIG/BRA delegation leader) Witnessed by: • BRA Commanders	Leslie Boseto (Minister for Home Affairs, Solomon Islands) **(Chairperson)**	• Hosted by Government of New Zealand • Financed by Government of Australia • Observers from Government of Solomon Islands	October 1997: The Burnham Truce marks the end of the 'War' on Bougainville. Following Burnham the BIG/BRA leadership moved to disassociate itself and operate independently from Francis Ona (who refuses to participate at Burnham or sign the Truce) under the leadership of Joseph Kabui and Sam Kauona
25	19–24 Nov 1997	24 Nov 1997	Cairns, Australia	The Cairns Commitment (including a Joint Press Statement)	• Agreement to establish and deploy a neutral TMG • Establishment of a Peace Consultative Committee (PCC) with core members from the National Government (3), BTG(2), BIG(2), BRA(2), BRF(2) • PCC is to review and assess implementation and adherence by the signatories to the Burnham Truce • Review commitment in January 1998 • Agenda set for next leaders meeting	• Kapeatu Puaria (BTG Legal Advisor) • Robert Igara (Secretary for Prime Minister)	Martin Miriori (BIG/BRA delegation leader)	Leslie Boseto (Minister for Home Affairs, Solomon Islands) **(Chairperson)**	Facilitated by: • Government of Australia Witnessed by: • The Hon. Rev. Leslie BOSETO (Minister for Home Affairs, Government of Solomon Islands) • David RITCHIE (Representative, Government of Australia) • Bede CORRY (Representative, Government of New Zealand)	5 December 1997: Agreement signed in Port Moresby between the Governments of PNG, Australia, Fiji, Vanuatu and New Zealand for the deployment of a TMG commencing 6 December 1997
26	19–23 Jan 1998	23 Jan 1998	Lincoln University, Christchurch, New Zealand	Lincoln Agreement	• Renounce violence and commit to achieving peace by peaceful means • Extension of the Burnham Truce to 30 April 1998	• John Kaputin (Chief Negotiator, PNG Government) • Sam Akoitai (Minister for Bougainville	• Joseph Kabui (BIG Vice President) • Sam Kauona (BRA Military Commander)	Bartholomew Ulufa'alu (Prime Minister, Solomon	Facilitated by: • Government of New Zealand In attendance: • Government leaders from Fiji	

Ser.	Period of Negotia-tion	Date of Agreement	Place of Agreement	Title of Agreement	Agreement	The Parties Key PNG Government/ Pro-PNG Government representatives	Leader—Bougainville Delegation	Chairperson/ Mediator/ Facilitator	3rd Party Involvement (Witnesses and Observers)	Post Agreement Events
					• Permanent and irrevocable ceasefire to take effect from 2400H on 30 April 1998 • Phased withdrawal of PNGDF and restoration of civil authority • Arrangements for deployment of a successor to the TMG (the Peace Monitoring Group (PMG)) to be finalised by 30 April 1998 • PNG to approach UN to request Observer Mission to oversee arrangements • Amnesty and Pardon for participants in the Crisis and a removal of 'bounties' on individuals • Promote reconciliation • Transition to civilian policing • Restoration of services on Bougainville • Promote public awareness and respect for the Agreement • Meet to discuss the political future of Bougainville before the end of June 1998	Affairs, PNG Government) • Gerard Sinato(BTG Premier) Other Bougainville Parliamentary Representatives from the PNG Government • Hilary Masiria (Resistance Commander)		Islands) **(Chairperson)**	• Government leaders from Vanuatu • Government leaders from New Zealand • Government leaders from Australia Observers: • Valery Marusin (Special Envoy of the Secretary-General of the UN)I	
27	27 Mar 1998	March 1998	Canberra, Australia	Technical Meeting (Supplementation of the Ceasefire Agreement)	• Further talks prior to Arawa and implementation of the Lincoln Agreement • Opportunity for all the parties to discuss details of the permanent ceasefire • Explore options for the level of external involvement in monitoring the peace process	• PNG Government • BRF	BRA/BIG		Facilitated by Government of Australia	• 22 April 1998: UN Security Council Announces Support for the Lincoln Agreement and calls on the UN Secretary-General to consider a UN Observer Mission on Bougainville • 29 April 1998: Protocol signed for establishment of PMG (a successor to the TMG) between PNG, Vanuatu, Fiji, New Zealand and Australia
28	30 April 1998	30 April 1998	Arawa, Bougainville	Arawa Agreement (annex 1 to the Lincoln Agreement)	• Implemented the Lincoln Agreement and permanent ceasefire • Established a Peace Process Consultative Committee (PPCC) that will be chaired by the leader of the UN Observer Mission or another person agreeable to the parties	• John Kaputin (Chief Negotiator, PNG Government) • Sam AKOITAI (Minister for Bougainville Affairs, PNG Government) • Gerard Sinato (BTG Premier) • Other Bougainville Parliamentary Representatives from the PNG Government • Hilary Masiria (BRF Chairman)	• Joseph Kabui (BIG Vice President) • Sam Kauona (BRA Military Commander)		Facilitated by: • TMG Witnessed by: • Bartholomew Ulufa'alu (Prime Minister, Solomon Islands) • Don McKinnon (NZ Minister for Foreign Affairs and Trade) • Alexander Downer (Australian Minister for Foreign Affairs) • Bernardo Vunibobo (Fiji Minister for Foreign Affairs) • Clement Leon (Acting Vanuatu Minister for Foreign Affairs) • Dr Francis Vendrell (Representative of the UN Secretary-General)	• 30 April 1998: TMG becomes Australian-led PMG • 2 June 1988: Letter from the UN Secretary-General to the President of the Security Council endorsing the deployment of a United Nations Observer Mission on Bougainville (UNOMB) • June 1998: Withdrawal of PNGDF from Arawa, Bougainville • June 1998: Bougainville Leaders Meeting to discuss arrangements for free and democratic elections for a Bougainville Reconciliation Government (BRG) to be established before the end of 1998. It also discussed autonomy and the deployment of a UN Observer Mission • 1 August 1998: United Nations Political Office in Bougainville becomes operational

Ser.	Period of Negotia-tion	Date of Agreement	Place of Agreement	Title of Agreement	Agreement	The Parties Key PNG Government/ Pro-PNG Government representatives	Leader—Bougainville Delegation	Chairperson/ Mediator/ Facilitator	3rd Party Involvement (Witnesses and Observers)	Post Agreement Events
29	20–22 Aug 1998	22 Aug 1998	Buin, Bougainville	Buin Declaration (Pan-Bougainville Leaders Conference)	• Confirmation that independence is the common goal for Bougainville to be achieved through peaceful means • Calls for establishment of BRG • Other issues including development and the disposal of arms to be raised at PPCC.		• Women of Bougainville • Chiefs of Central, South and North Bougainville	Reverend Leslie Beseto (Minister for Home Affairs & Chairman of Solomon Islands Bougainville Peace Committee, Government of Solomon Islands) **(Chairperson)**		7–8 October 1998: First meeting of the PPCC chaired by Valery Marusin (UN Representative). Observers at the PPCC meeting include the Commander PMG and representatives from Australia, New Zealand, Fiji and Vanuatu
30	24 Dec 1998	24 Dec 1998	Arawa, Bougainville	Draft Basic Agreement Concerning the Bougainville Reconciliation Government	• Detail a proposed constitution for the BRG • Detail establishment, principles and structure of BRG	• PNG Government • BTG leaders • BRF leaders	BIG/BRA Leaders			• 1998: MP John Momis creates a new grouping (the Leitana Council of Elders) which included the local-level government for the island of Buka and senior leaders of the BRF • December 1998: Legislation to establish the BRG fails to pass second reading. It is proposed that the new Interim Government due to be established in January 1999 will be suspended to make way for an Interim BRG • 31 December 1998: BTG Charter expires and in the absence of enabling legislation (to establishment a BRG), the default position is the re-instatement of the Bougainville Provincial Government on the same status as all other PNG provinces (John Momis would become Governor of Bougainville as Member for Bougainville Regional in the national parliament) • January 1999: Interim Provincial Government arrangements commence and the PNG Government suspends the BTG and places the province under National Executive Council control (John Momis mounts a constitutional challenge to the suspension) • 15 January 1999: Bougainville Constituent Assembly (BCA) elected (Joseph Kabui (BIG vice-chairman) and Gerard Sinato (former BTG Premier) elected as Co-Chairmen). The BCA is responsible for drawing up a constitution for the interim form of BRG to be called the Bougainville People's Congress (BPC) and for an advisory role to the NEC until the body is elected
31	14–22 April 1999	22 April 1999	Lake Okataina, New Zealand	Matakana and Okataina Understanding (to resolve differences stemming from the December 1998 interim political arrangements for Bougainville)	• Pledge to maintain the permanent and irrevocable ceasefire and peaceful negotiation on the political future of Bougainville • The four Bougainville MPs must work together (united political leadership) • Special State Negotiator will prepare a package of proposals on the powers, functions, structure and status of Bougainville's government, geared to Bougainville's needs. All individuals and groups in Bougainville will be given the opportunity to make written submissions to the Special State Negotiator	The Government of PNG Four Members of the National Parliament	The Bougainville Constituent Assembly (BCA) Leitana Council of Elders		Facilitated by: • Government of New Zealand Witnessed by: • Paul Reeves, (Archbishop and Primate of New Zealand (1980–85) and former Governor-General of New Zealand (1985-90))	28 May 1999: Bougainville People's Congress (BPC) Inauguration Ceremony in Arawa under Joseph Kabui (primarily comprising members of the BIG)

Ser.	Period of Negotiation	Date of Agreement	Place of Agreement	Title of Agreement	Agreement	The Parties Key PNG Government/ Pro-PNG Government representatives	Leader—Bougainville Delegation	Chairperson/ Mediator/ Facilitator	3rd Party Involvement (Witnesses and Observers)	Post Agreement Events
					• Request that the technical officers of the Bougainvillean parties meet as soon as possible to prepare for discussions on future arrangements for government on Bougainville, including discussions on other related matters raised in this document • Political leaders will meet to discuss the package as soon as possible, and no later than 30 June 1999 • Weapons disposal should begin immediately under UNOMB and New Zealand supervision • Work toward establishment of a Provincial Government • For the purposes of transparency and accountability, all future negotiations should take place in Bougainville or PNG					
32	30 June 1999	30 June 1999	Rabaul, New Britain	Fundamental Principles for the Future of Bougainville	• Addressed the issue of the future political status of Bougainville • Prime Minister undertook to submit the 'Fundamental principles' prepared by the BPC to the National Executive Council for its consideration • The Prime Minister of PNG advised that the Government would be prepared to consider the proposal for a referendum for independence • The meeting accepted that Bougainville should be given a status under which Bougainville will exercise the powers of government with the exception of certain powers to be negotiated that shall be retained by the Government of Papua New Guinea • Agreement that every effort should be made to build bipartisan support for the agreements to be reached between the parties • The parties shall meet as soon as practicable to further these discussions	Bill Skate (PNG Prime Minister)	Mr Joseph Kabui (President BPC)		Witnessed by: • David Irvine (High Commissioner for Australia) • Maria Mataeva (Deputy High Commissioner for Fiji) • Nigel Moore (High Commissioner for New Zealand) • LTCOL Clyde Parris (UN Observer Mission in Bougainville) • Brigadier Simon Willis (Australian Commander, PMG, Bougainville)	

Ser.	Period of Negotia-tion	Date of Agreement	Place of Agreement	Title of Agreement	Agreement	The Parties Key PNG Government/ Pro-PNG Government representatives	Leader—Bougainville Delegation	Chairperson/ Mediator/ Facilitator	3rd Party Involvement (Witnesses and Observers)	Post Agreement Events
33	10 July 1999	10 July 1999	Port Moresby, New Guinea	Hutjena Minute	Submission of the 'Fundamental Principles' document signed on 30 June 1999 to the National Executive Council for consideration	Bill Skate (PNG Prime Minister)	Mr Joseph Kabui (President BPC)		Witnessed by: • Noel Sinclair (UN Observer Mission) • Brigadier Frank Roberts (Commander PMG)	14 July 1999: Mekere Morauta replaces Bill Skate as PM of PNG
34	14–15 Dec 1999	15 Dec 1999	Buka, Bougainville	Hutjena Record	• Bougainville Delegation presented a document recording Bougainville's common view as to the future of Bougainville, and noted that the people of Bougainville are of the firm conviction that the issues of Autonomy and Referendum are inseparably linked and must be considered together • The PNG Minister undertook to make a submission on the issue of Referendum as outlined in the Bougainville Parties 'Joint Bougainville Negotiating • Position' to the National Executive Council for its consideration • Government of Papua New Guinea agrees that the highest possible Autonomy for Bougainville, subject to negotiation • Government shall at the same time provide its response to the principle of Referendum as outlined in the Bougainville proposal • The Parties shall meet before the end of January 2000 to consider the responses of the Government of Papua New Guinea	Michael Somare (On behalf of PNG Government Delegation—Minister for Bougainville Affairs and Chairman of the National Committee on Bougainville)	• Joseph Kabui (BPC President, on behalf of Bougainville Delegation) • John Momis (Governor, on behalf of Bougainville Delegation)		Witnessed by: • Noel Sinclair (UN Observers Mission) • Brigadier Frank ROBERTS (Australian Commander PMG)	• November 1999: John Momis wins his Constitutional challenge in the High Court and becomes Governor of the BIPG • 9 December 1999: John Momis is reinstated as Governor of Bougainville
35	23 Dec 1999	23 Dec 1999	Arawa, Bougainville	Greenhouse Memorandum	Finalise the relationship and arrangements between the BPC, the Bougainville Interim Provincial Government and the Leitana Council of Elders	BPC, BIPG and Leitana Council of Elders			Witnessed by: • Ambassador Noel Sinclair (UN Observers Mission) • BRIG Frank Roberts (Australian Commander PMG)	29 December 1999: A local ceremony is held at Buka, initiated by the Leitana Council of Elders, to reinstall John Momis as Governor. Joseph Kabui attended as BPC President
36	17–23 March 2000	23 March 2000	Loloata Island, Central Province and Islander Hotel, Port Moresby, PNG	Loloata Understanding	• Reaffirmed commitment to the peace process, and to consultation and cooperation within the framework and spirit of the Lincoln Agreement • The parties discussed the Bougainville paper, 'Bougainville Common Negotiating Position: Expanded Details' dated 8 March 2000, and the Papua New Guinea Government paper,	Michael Somare (Minister for Bougainville Affairs and Chairman of the National Committee on Bougainville)	• John Momis (Governor, Co-Leader of the Bougainville Delegation) • Joel Banam (Chairman, Leitana Council of Elders)		Witnessed by: • Noel Sinclair (Director of the UN Observer Mission) • Ewan McMillan (Chief Negotiator, PMG)	30 March 2000: Bougainville Interim Provincial Government (BIPG) sworn in by the PNG Governor-General at Buka

Ser.	Period of Negotia-tion	Date of Agreement	Place of Agreement	Title of Agreement	Agreement	The Parties Key PNG Government/ Pro-PNG Government representatives	Leader—Bougainville Delegation	Chairperson/ Mediator/ Facilitator	3rd Party Involvement (Witnesses and Observers)	Post Agreement Events
					'The National Delegation's Position on the Bougainville Delegation's Autonomy Proposals' dated 19 March 2000, and other papers, and agreed that these documents provide for future negotiations between the parties • Establishment of a Bougainville Interim Provincial Government (BIPG) • Movement toward autonomous government • Referendum on independence following autonomy		• Joseph Kabui (BPC President, Co-Leader of the Bougainville Delegation)			
37	23 May–9 June 2000	9 June 2000	Gateway Hotel, Port Moresby, PNG	Gateway Communiqué	• Bougainville Delegation presented the National Government Delegation with a detailed working paper called 'Proposals for a Special Status Agreement', outlining the proposed draft of an agreement between the parties on a political settlement (based on a document entitled 'Autonomy and Referendum', which the National Government Delegation has accepted as the basis for further negotiations • The parties agreed that these documents would provide the basis for future negotiations • Discussed issues such as capacity building, institutional strengthening, weapons disposal, amnesty and pardon, withdrawal of security forces and reconstruction of infrastructure, restoration of services and development • It was agreed that the PPCC shall meet as soon as possible to develop proposals for weapons disposal and the phased withdrawal of the PNG security forces • The parties agreed on additional time to negotiate details of the agreement • Agreement to begin further exchanges concerning all the above issues no later than the first week of July 2000 (a final agreement is to be concluded no later than mid-September 2000)	Michael Somare (Minister for Bougainville Affairs and Chairman of the National Committee on Bougainville)	• John Momis (Governor BIPG and Co-Leader of the Bougainville Delegation) • Joseph Kabui (BPC President and Co-Leader of the Bougainville Delegation)		Witnessed by: • Brigadier M. Silverstone (Commander, PMG) • Scott Smith (UN Observer Mission)	• February 2001: Weapons Disposal Talks conducted between Bougainville leaders and the PNG Government in Townsville • 26 January 2001: Agreed principles on deferred conditional referendum on independence, initialed at Kokopo, PNG • March 2001: Autonomy talks conducted between Bougainville leaders and the PNG Government in Port Moresby • 4–6 July 2000: National Government Bougainville policy workshop in Port Moresby

Ser.	Period of Negotiation	Date of Agreement	Place of Agreement	Title of Agreement	Agreement	The Parties Key PNG Government/ Pro-PNG Government representatives	Leader—Bougainville Delegation	Chairperson/ Mediator/ Facilitator	3rd Party Involvement (Witnesses and Observers)	Post Agreement Events
38	7–19 July 2000	No agreement	Gateway Hotel, Port Moresby, PNG	Bougainville and National Government technical talks	Talks in accordance with the Gateway Communiqué	PNG Government	Bougainville Leaders			July 2000–May 2001: Talks stall over details of autonomy
39	Aug–Sept 2000	11 Sept 2000	Rabaul, New Britain, PNG	Record of Outcome of Political Talks between Bougainville Leaders and National Government	• Autonomy • Referendum • Arms disposal	PNG Government	Bougainville Leaders			December 2000: Moi Avei replaces Michael Somare as Minister for Bougainville Affairs
40	Oct 2000–Jan 2001	26 Jan 2001	Kopoko, New Britain, PNG	Kopoko Agreement (Agreed Principles on Referendum)	Agreed principles on a referendum for Bougainville independence within 15 years (and no earlier than 10 years) of the election of a Bougainville Autonomous Government (BAG) unless that government decides not to conduct such a referendum	Moi Avei (Minister for Bougainville Affairs)	Bougainville Leaders	Noel Sinclair (Director UNOMB) **(Chairperson)**	Witnessed by: • Dr Stephen Henningham (Chief Negotiator, PMG)	
41	Feb–April 2001	19–26 Feb 2001 (Talks broke down)	Townsville, Australia	Record of Official Discussions on Autonomy Arrangements for Bougainville	Autonomy arrangements for Bougainville	Moi Avei (Minister for Bougainville Affairs)	Bougainville Leaders	Nick Warner (Australian High Commissioner to PNG) **(Facilitator)**	Facilitated by: • Government of Australia: • PMG)	
42		March–April 2001	Gateway Hotel and Port Moresby, PNG	Joint Work in Progress on Autonomy—Including recommended Text to be Incorporated in Townsville Record						
43	1–3 May 2001	3 May 2001	Togarau, Bougainville	Rotokas Record	• BRA and BRF commit to the development of peace, democracy and the restoration of fundamental human rights without the threat or the use of weapons • To a three phase Weapons Disposal Plan (Surrender, containment and verification, and decision on final fate of weapons)	Hilary Masiria (BRF Chairman)	Ishmael Toroama (BRA Chief of Defence)		Witnessed by: • Noel Sinclair (UN Observer Mission) • Matt Anderson (Negotiator, PMG)	
44	7–9 May 2001	9 May 2001	Buka, Bougainville	PPCC Resolution on Weapons Disposal	• PPCC meeting on disposal of weapons • PPCC welcomes the arrangements in the Rotokas Record • Reaffirm commitment to Lincoln Agreement • Develop PPCC sub-committee to oversee weapons disposal arrangements: Chairman—Director UNOMB or	• PNG Government PPCC members led by William Dihm • Hilary Masiria (BRF Chairman) • Bougainville Joint Technical Team	Ishmael Toroama (BRA Chief of Defence)		Witnessed by: • Noel Sinclair (UN Observer Mission) • Brigadier Michael SWAN (Commander PMG)	29 August 2001: Joint Bougainville Negotiating Team releases a statement titled 'Bougainville Peace Agreement—Summary of Aims and Contents'

Ser.	Period of Negotiation	Date of Agreement	Place of Agreement	Title of Agreement	Agreement	The Parties Key PNG Government/ Pro-PNG Government representatives	Leader—Bougainville Delegation	Chairperson/ Mediator/ Facilitator	3rd Party Involvement (Witnesses and Observers)	Post Agreement Events
					representative; Deputy Chairman—Commander PMG or representative					
45	22–25 June 2001	25 June 2001	Gateway Hotel, Port Moresby, PNG	Agreed Basis for a Comprehensive Political Settlement between the Parties to the Bougainville peace process	The document outlines the arrangements for the establishment of an autonomous Bougainville government, including provisions for a Bougainville-specific police force and conditions for the redeployment of the PNGDF	PNG Government	All parties (except Francis Ona)			
46	30 Aug 2001	30 Aug 2001	Arawa, Bougainville	Bougainville Peace Agreement	• High level of autonomy for Bougainville • Referendum to be held on independence within 15 years of the election of the Bougainville Autonomous Government • Amendments to be made to the PNG Constitution to accommodate agreement • Weapons disposal and adoption of the 'PPCC Resolution on Weapons Disposal' of 9 May 2001 • Withdrawal of Security Forces • Arrangements for peace monitoring	• Mekere MORAUTA (Prime Minister of PNG) • Hilary Masiria (BRF Chairman)	• John Momis (BIPG Governor) • Joseph Kabui (BPC President) • Ishmael Toroama (BRA Chief of Defence)		Witnessed by: representatives of: • Government of New Zealand • Government of Australia • Government of Fiji • Government of Vanuatu • Government of Solomon Islands • UN Observer Mission • PMG	• 31 August 2001: Joint Bougainville Negotiating Team releases a statement titled Bougainville Interim Provincial Government and Bougainville People's Congress 'Implementing the Bougainville Peace Agreement' • 31 October 2001: UN Mandate for UNPOB extended to chairing the weapons disposal sub-committee • 6 December 2001: First of many weapons surrender and containment ceremonies takes place on Bougainville • 27 March 2002: PNG Parliament approves Constitutional amendments to give effect to Peace Agreement • 2003–2004: BRA 'A' Company (but not remainder of Francis Ona's MDF) joins the peace process and disarms by 6 May 2004 • 1 February 2003: First draft Bougainville Constitution released for consultation • 25 March 2003: Second draft Bougainville Constitution released for consultation • 17 April 2003: Last PNGDF elements depart Bougainville • 23 July 2003: PMG departs Bougainville and is replaced by a small civilian Bougainville Transitional Team (BTT) • 25 July 2003: UNPOB confirms weapon containment is complete • 7 August 2003: PNG Constitutional amendments allowing for Bougainville autonomy take effect • 17 December 2003: PPCC decided that all contained weapons would be destroyed • 31 December 2003: BTT departs Bougainville • 1 January 2004: UNPOB is replaced by a smaller UN Observer Mission Bougainville (UNOMB) • 20 April 2005: John Momis resigns as Governor (Gerard Sinato is Acting Governor until 15 June 2005) • 6 May 2005: UNCMB reports that destruction is nearing completion and that the conditions were now stable enough for BAG elections to occur • 20 May–2 June 2005: BAG elections are conducted supervised by an International election Observer Mission • 15 June 2005: 39 member BAG is elected to be led by President Joseph Kabui • 30 June 2005: Mandate for UNOMB ends • 24 July 2005: Francis Ona Dies • 5 August 2002: Michael Somare replaces Mekere Morauta as PM of PNG

Fisher, R., 'Negotiating With the Russians and With Your Spouse: Is There a Difference?', Harvard Negotiation Project, Harvard University, Cambridge, MA, 10 August 1988, available at <http://www.pon.harvard.edu/hnp/PDF/spouse.pdf>, accessed 31 March 2009

Hassall, G., 'Peace Agreements in the Pacific Islands', in *Regional Workshop on Conflict Prevention and Peace-building in the Pacific*, Pacific Islands Forum Secretariat, Nadi, United Nations Department of Political Affairs, 25–27 April 2005

Limbury, A., 'Principled Negotiation and Constructive Mediation', Seminar Paper: 'Negotiation Skills for Lawyers', Centre for Continuing Education, Faculty of Law, University of New South Wales, 4 August 2005

Menkel-Meadow, C., 'Lawyer Negotiations: Theories and Realities-What we Learn from Mediation', *Modern Law Review*, vol. 56, no. 3, May 1993, p. 367

Miriori, M., 'A Bougainville Interim Government (BIG) Perspective on Early Peace Efforts', in A. Carl and L. Garasu (eds), *Weaving Consensus: The Papua New Guinea—Bougainville peace process* (Accord issue 12, 2002), available at <http://www.c-r.org/our-work/accord/png-bougainville/big-perspective.php>, accessed 31 March 2009

Nathan, L., 'Undue Pressure: International Mediation in Africa Civil Wars', in L. Reychler and T. Paffenholz, *Peace Building: A Field Guide*, Lynne Rienner, Boulder, CO, 2001

Patterson, K., 'Australia Promotes Gender Equality and Peace-Building', in *Focus*, Canberra, March 2001, available at <http://www.womenwarpeace.org/webfm_send/92>, accessed 31 March 2009

Regan, A.J., 'Phases in the Negotiation Process', in A. Carl and L. Garasu (eds), *Weaving Consensus: The Papua New Guinea—Bougainville peace process* (Accord issue 12, 2002), available at <http://www.c-r.org/our-work/accord/png-bougainville/phases.php>, accessed 31 March 2009

Saovana-Spriggs, R., 'Bougainville Women's Role in Conflict Resolution in the Bougainville Peace Process' in S. Dinnen, A. Jowitt, and Cain T. Newton Cain (eds), *A Kind of Mending: Restorative Justice in the Pacific Islands*, Pandanus Books, Canberra, 2003

Sohia, P., 'Early Interventions', in A. Carl and L. Garasu (eds), *Weaving Consensus: The Papua New Guinea—Bougainville peace process* (Accord issue 12, 2002), available at <http://www.c-r.org/our-work/accord/png-bougainville/early-interventions.php>, accessed 31 March 2009

Smith, W.P., 'Effectiveness of the Biased Mediator', *Negotiation Journal*, vol. 1, no. 4, 2 July 2007, pp. 363–72

Tapi, R., 'From Burnham to Buin: Sowing the Seeds of Peace in the Land of the Snow Capped Mountains', in A. Carl and L. Garasu, *Weaving Consensus: The Papua New Guinea—Bougainville peace process* (Accord issue 12, 2002), available at <http://www.c-r.org/our-work/accord/png-bougainville/burnham-buin.php>, accessed 31 March 2009

Wolfers, E.P., *International Peace Missions In Bougainville, Papua New Guinea, 1990–2005: Host State Perceptions*, Regional Forum on Reinventing Government Exchange and Transfer of Innovations for Transparent Governance and State Capacity, Nadi, 20-22 February 2006

Bibliography

Books

Astor, H. and Chinkin, C., *Dispute Resolution in Australia* (2nd ed.), LexisNexis Butterworths, Sydney, 2002

Bowd, R.R.E., *Doves Over the Pacific: In Pursuit of Peace and Stability in Bougainville*, Australian Military History Publications, Sydney, 1997

Brandon, M. and Robertson, L., *Conflict and Dispute Resolution: A Guide for Practice*, Oxford University Press, Melbourne, 2007

Burton, J.W., *Conflict Resolution: Its Language and Processes*, Scarecrow Press, Lanham, MD, 1996

Fisher, R., *Basic Negotiating Strategy: International Conflict for Beginners*, Penguin Press, London, 1971

———, *Beyond Machiavelli: Tools for Coping with Conflict*, Penguin Books, New York, 1996

Fisher, R. and Brown, S., *Getting Together: Building a Relationship that Gets to* Yes, Houghton Mifflin Company, Boston, 1988

Fisher, R. and Ertel, D., *Getting Ready To Negotiate: the Getting to Yes Workbook*, Penguin Books, New York, 1995

Fisher, R. and Ury, W. *Getting to Yes: Negotiating Agreements Without Giving In*, Random House, London, 1992

Frei, D., *Managing International Crises*, Sage Publications, California, 1982

Le Poole, S., *Never Take No For An Answer: A Guide to Successful Negotiation*, Kogan Page, London, 1987

Lewicki, R.J., Saunders, D.M., Minton, J.M. and Barry, B., *Negotiation: Readings. Exercises and Cases* (4th ed.), McGraw-Hill, New York, 2003

Mayer, B.S., *Beyond Neutrality: Confronting the Crisis in Conflict* Resolution, Jossey-Bass, San Francisco, 2004

National Alternative Dispute Resolution Advisory Council, *Alternative Dispute Resolution Definitions*, NADRAC, Canberra, 1997a

Oliver, D., *Black Islanders: A Personal Perspective of Bougainville 1937–1991*, Hyland House, Melbourne, 1991

Regan, A., *Bougainville: The Peace Process and Beyond*, Submission to the Foreign Affairs Sub-Committee of the Joint Standing Committee on Foreign Affairs, Defence and Trade Inquiry, Canberra, June 1999, available at <http://www.aph.gov.au/house/committee/jfadt/bougainville/BVrepindx.htm>, accessed 31 March 2009.

Report of the Visit of the Australian Parliamentary Delegation to Bougainville 18–22 April 1994, *Bougainville: A Pacific Solution*, Australian Government Publishing Service, Canberra, 1994

The Challenges Project, *Challenges of Peace Operations: Into the 21st Century—Concluding Report: 1997–2002*, Elanders Gotab, Stockholm, 2002

Tillett, G., *Resolving Conflict: A Practical Approach* (2nd ed.), Oxford University Press, Melbourne, 1999

Ury, W., *Getting Past No: Negotiating With Difficult People*, Random House, London, 1991

Articles, book chapters and Internet resources

Bercovitch, J., 'International Mediation and Intractable Conflict', January 2004, available at <http://www.beyondintractability.org/essay/med_intractable_conflict/>, accessed 31 March 2009

Burnham II Preparatory Talks, Burnham Military Camp, New Zealand, 1–10 October 1997, *Record of Understanding* (dated 10 October 1997)

Eagles, J., 'Aid as an Instrument for Peace: A Civil Society Perspective', in A. Carl and L. Garasu (eds), *Weaving Consensus: The Papua New Guinea—Bougainville peace process* (Accord issue 12, 2002), available at <http://www.c-r.org/our-work/accord/png-bougainville/aid.php>, accessed 31 March 2009

Emmerig, J., 'Advanced Negotiation for Lawyers: Tricks and Traps in Negotiation', August 2005 (unpublished)